From the Mountain's Edge

Also by Ed Jackson

Lucky

From the Mountain's Edge

Ed Jackson

HQ

ONE PLACE. MANY STORIES

HQ
An imprint of HarperCollins*Publishers* Ltd
1 London Bridge Street
London SE1 9GF

www.harpercollins.co.uk

HarperCollins*Publishers*
Macken House, 39/40 Mayor Street Upper,
Dublin 1, D01 C9W8, Ireland

This edition 2025

1

First published in Great Britain by HQ,
an imprint of HarperCollins*Publishers* Ltd 2025

HB ISBN:978-0-00-873536-4
TPB ISBN: 978-0-00-873535-7

This book is set in Sabon by Type-it AS, Norway

Printed and bound in the UK using 100% Renewable
Electricity by CPI Group (UK) Ltd

FSC
www.fsc.org

MIX
Paper
FSC™ C007454

For more information visit: www.harpercollins.co.uk/green

For Lois –

Your love, strength and quiet courage have
guided me through every climb, on the mountain
and off. I wouldn't be here without you.

The Summit

I have died before. Three times, in fact.

When I broke my neck diving into a pool, the ambulance journey between hospitals took two hours longer than anticipated. My family was left waiting for my arrival at the hospital, their hopes fading.

I was lucky that day as there was a doctor in the back of the ambulance. He helped the paramedic bring me back to life after my heart stopped three times. Together, they dosed me full of adrenaline and pumped my heart when it couldn't beat by itself.

But that experience of death was very different from the one I am now facing.

We are just a few hundred metres below the summit of Himlung Himal in Nepal. The sun is shining brightly, but we cannot move either up or down as hidden crevasses surround us, each covered by thick, fluffy snow that didn't freeze last night. We will only know if the drop the snow hides is one metre or 100 when we step on it. There is no route through the brilliant white of the crevasse field and there isn't a medic with us. We are trapped and cannot go any further.

We don't have any water, shelter or food. We haven't slept for thirty-six hours and our bodies are battered and bruised from the days of gruelling climbs. We only have one of our mountain guides with us and it is just the five of us left. No one could have predicted this set of circumstances and they couldn't have been prevented. Some days the mountains just won't let you pass. I know what we are facing up here could easily take us as close to death as I had been in that ambulance after my accident.

The natural adrenaline racing around my body after everything that has happened in the past few hours is wearing off.

I begin to shake uncontrollably. Full body judders that are impossible to hide. I pull deep into myself, becoming less aware of my surroundings and more focused on my breathing and racing heartbeat. It is a mental game now, one where I have to stop my mind from tipping me over into terror. One of my friends helps me to sit, while the other leans away from us and vomits. It is tinged with blood. I hope that if it is altitude sickness, it doesn't develop into high-altitude pulmonary edema, which is life-threatening.

I can't control my body as it continues to shake. Even with my fogged mind, I know I am going into shock. I peer at my friends through the small slit left for my eyes between the insulated hat pulled down over my eyebrows and the seamless material of the buff that covers my mouth all the way up to the bridge of my nose. We are all clearly exhausted. Someone hands me an oxygen mask, but my body won't respond to the simple signal I send to reach out to it. I can't move my arms to take the mask, just like when I was paralyzed at the bottom of the pool and couldn't push myself to the surface.

A few metres away, I hear the beeps of the satnav phone.

Bigraj speaks into it in Nepali, moving further away from us to try and get a clear signal.

Relief floods through me that the decision has been made

to call in a helicopter and help is on its way. In all my years of climbing, I have never needed to have a helicopter sent out, but I know there isn't any other option. Someone pulls the mask onto my face as my body continues to judder. I imagine the oxygen flooding my veins and filling my muscles, travelling around the corners of my body that have been starved of it for so long. The beep of the satnav phone and muffled conversation reassure me that we are not alone.

I can feel myself wanting to sleep again even though it is still daylight, just as I had in the back of the ambulance five years ago. I can see it in my friends' hunched forms. We are all struggling to stay awake, but we know falling asleep without a tent is how you die at these altitudes. Your core temperature drops when you sleep and that is something we can't risk getting any lower when we will soon be subjected to temperatures of around -25°C. We will have to burrow into ourselves, drawing on our last reserves for another hour or two while waiting for the helicopter to arrive.

Bigraj picks his way over to us in the knee-high snow and begins to speak. I follow his lips but cannot trace the words.

Dazed, I pull the mask from my face, relieved my arms are working again. 'Say it again.'

'We must wait until morning,' he repeats. 'The sun will set any minute. The helicopters cannot fly at night because the mountains are too high here. They say they cannot make it before it gets dark.'

'Is there nothing we can do to make them change their minds?'

Before he answers, I already know it is pointless. They would come if they could.

'No, nothing can change their minds. Even when they set off in the morning, the highest most helicopters can fly is 6,000 metres. So, it is good we have already come down this far. In the morning, I will try to find a safe landing spot for them.'

Questions circle my mind. Would the snow freeze overnight to cover the crevasses and enable us to cross them? Was the pilot experienced in landing so high? Would the helicopter be stripped back so it is light enough to reach us?

I roll onto my side and stare at the heavy orange sun beginning to set just above the mountains. Sunset and sunrise happen more quickly here as we are closer to the equator. Once the sun travels below the mountains, we will plunge into -25°C for twelve hours. My hands and feet have been numb for hours and I imagine it creeping up my arms and legs, meeting in the middle.

I haven't given up. None of us have, but the responsibility for my friends' safety weighs heavily on me; I'm the reason they are here. No one else was in danger when I had dived into that pool and there was no risk of taking anyone else with me. But it is not just me who has to get through the night. My friends do as well and the chances of survival are slim. To try and keep myself and the others awake, I begin to hum one of the songs that had helped me through the long weeks in a hospital bed.

The sun slips below the horizon, leaving us to the night.

CHAPTER 1

'Don't bring right kit. Lose toe.'

As I hummed Bob Marley's 'Three Little Birds', I surveyed the mound of socks on the bed that I needed for my impending expedition up Himlung Himal in Nepal. The flight was the following morning and, as was my usual approach, I'd left packing until the day before despite it taking me longer than most people to do. It's not easy to roll socks when your hands curl around and your fingers have lost their dexterity, but I was mid-kit muster and staring at the pile wasn't going to get the task done. At least Bob was keeping me company – one of the many musicians who had helped me through my lowest points after the diving accident in which I had broken my neck five years ago. Curled hands were one of the many things the accident had left me with, along with a significant limp and many other muddled messages between my brain and body, but I would take that any day over the possible loss of nearly all the movement below my neck, which was my original prognosis.

I joined in with Bob as the reggae beats filled the cottage in Somerset where I lived with my wife, Lois.

First sock set done, I surveyed what was left. Spread out across our bed was everything I should need to get up a 7,000-metre mountain and, equally importantly, back down again. If I could do this, I would be one of the first two people with spinal cord injuries to reach that height. Ben, a beneficiary of the charity I had founded with Lois, was also joining me on this expedition and I was hoping we would achieve this record together. Our charity, Millimetres 2 Mountains, was designed to help beneficiaries with their mental health through the healing powers of the outdoors. We had established a programme that began with a walking or trekking challenge that would redefine their limitations, followed by ongoing support through life coaching, funding for therapy or career grants. Ben was one of these beneficiaries and had been on several day-long walks with us already. He had also kindly offered to fundraise on this trip for a spinal injury hospital in Nepal that we had supported for years.

We'd also promised the trip's sponsor, Berghaus, some great footage while I tested out the new kit adaptations I'd been working on with them. We hoped it would help get more people with physical limitations into the outdoors and having adventures. This is my mission in life: to show people of all backgrounds the restorative potential of these hiking and mountaineering adventures. There is nothing quite like them to put your life into perspective and I had witnessed their transformative power countless times on the regular expeditions I had organized.

This wasn't my first rodeo when it came to climbing mountains and I hoped we would get some unique footage for Berghaus to thank them for their sponsorship. Two weeks ago, when we should have been finalising our plans, we'd hit a giant snag – our videographer unexpectedly pulled out. So, the only option was to scrabble around to try and find a replacement. Our new videographer, Beetle, made the grade as he was brilliantly talented and physically fit. Also, because he was in his early twenties, he was able to drop everything to accompany a random guy from Instagram up a mountain. He ticked every box, apart from being untested at these heights – he'd only done long treks before and scaled Ben Nevis, which is a fifth of the height of the mountain we were due to tackle. We'd just have to see how he got on with the altitude and work out what to do if it became a problem.

I carried on rolling socks: a couple of lighter pairs for the hike up to around 4,000 metres and four pairs for the higher altitude. I had chosen merino wool as it is thick and warm but also dries quickly, therefore avoiding having to choose between damp, clean socks or dry, dirty ones, neither of which is particularly appealing. Debilitating blisters can be a real issue for any climber, but particularly for me as I can't feel any pain in my right leg and foot because I have been left with Brown-Séquard syndrome. This is a neurological condition that means I have weakness in one side of my body and sensation loss in the other. Not feeling any pain might initially sound like a win that will give you a competitive edge, but in reality it means I can miss the early tell-tale signs that I need to stop or adjust something. Consequently, I've rubbed some pretty monumental holes in my feet in the past. So, socks are always top of my list.

A few years ago, in my early climbing days, I had been taught to use a system from the navy called a kit muster, where you spread everything out before you start packing, make a check-list and tick everything off as it goes in your mountaineering rucksack and kit holdall. Consequently, every bit of our bed was taken up with my carefully laid-out belongings and they also flowed onto the floor. Clothes were in one corner and progressed from under layers right through to my thick, down jacket. Electronic equipment, such as battery packs, chargers and leads, was in another corner. Then there was my mountaineering equipment, including a helmet, harness, crampons and ice axe. Mountaineers typically do their kit muster a week before leaving to ensure they don't forget anything. I usually do it the day before I have to take a flight. With the climbs I had completed I thought I could safely call myself a mountaineer, but I was still working on being the most organized one.

Bigraj, the Nepalese expedition organizer I had entrusted with my life many times, had emailed the kit list and I had spent the morning in the attic happily pulling down everything I needed for this trip. Nothing makes me feel more alive and further from my accident than scaling some of the world's highest mountains and the anticipation for my next climb was building.

Every mountain requires different kit and, from experience, I was able to add a few items to the list myself. What perhaps made my list a bit more unusual was the pile of catheter bags, Conveens, which help collect urine, and other medical equipment I had to take with me, as this wasn't the type of thing you could easily pick up in Nepal. Spinal injuries like mine affect the signals sent from your brain to the rest of your body, so that was why my hands curled, my left foot didn't lift fully and I couldn't feel pain in my right leg. Among some of my scrambled signals was the one to my bladder, which had become unruly.

Downstairs, the front door opened and closed. Lois must have arrived back from walking our bulldog, Barry. I could hear his claws skittering along the hallway towards the stairs as he panted up them to see me. He lolloped into the bedroom, tongue hanging out the side of his mouth.

'Come here, Baz,' I said as I bent down to greet him with equal enthusiasm, scratching behind both of his ears.

He closed his eyes and accepted the fuss. Baz had clearly missed me as I'd been in Beijing to join the Channel 4 presenting team for the Winter Paralympics. I had only been back for a couple of nights and now I would be away again for another three weeks in Nepal.

I'd had Baz for years, and he'd taken a while to adjust to my change in career. Before my accident, I had been a professional rugby player since I was a teenager and played my first professional game at nineteen for Bath. My career had taken me to the Doncaster Knights, London Welsh, Wasps, and finally, the Dragons in Wales. Partway through, we decided to welcome a Bulldog puppy called Barry to the family who, after annoying her for a few months, became thick as thieves with my older Boxer dog Molly.

But then, when I was twenty-eight, I was thrown a curveball. I was at a family friend's house when I decided I fancied a quick dip and dived into their swimming pool. What I hadn't realized was that it was the shallow end, and I nearly severed my spinal cord. The diagnosis was quadriplegia, and the prognosis was bleak – I was told I would probably never walk again. Baz had to get used to spending three months away from me while I was in hospital, and once I learnt to walk, I had to find a new career. Luck was on my side, and after giving a talk about my accident, I was scouted to present rugby for Channel 4. More opportunities came from that, but they took me away from home for longer each year. Something Baz was finding hard to forgive.

When he'd had enough fuss, Baz made a couple of brief

attempts to jump on the bed – barely getting his chin over the side with his back legs scrabbling for purchase – until I gave in and helped him up. He settled down on my high-altitude jacket. Smart boy, it was definitely a lot cosier than my hiking boots.

Standing proudly next to my bed was something I had never needed before – a majestic pair of 8,000-metre climbing boots. What partly spurred my recovery was setting myself the goal of climbing Snowdon (Yr Wyddfa) on the first-year anniversary of my accident. What was supposed to have been a one-off way of marking the end of a chapter in my life turned into the prologue. That one small climb sparked something inside me, and now, two or three times a year, I would be heading skyward.

I sat down next to the boots and lifted one to inspect it, surprised at how lightweight they were. These high-altitude boots were 40 cm of fresh-out-the-box insulation and would take up half a holdall. They were the boots you would climb Everest in. Himlung Himal is just over 7,000 metres high, about 2,000 metres lower than Everest but a notoriously cold mountain as it is very exposed. These gaitered below-the-knee beauties would hopefully protect me from frostbite, which is something I'm even more susceptible to following the accident as the circulation in my left leg isn't so good because of decreased muscle tone, meaning the warm blood doesn't reach my extremities as easily on that side. Bigraj's sage words to me on our first mountaineering journey up Mera Peak three years ago had always stayed with me: 'People think it easy, don't bring right kit. Lose toe.'

'Are you admiring your boots again?' Lois asked as she came into the bedroom, holding a plate piled high with thick slices of freshly buttered sourdough she had baked that morning. Lois had developed a recent obsession with baking the perfect sourdough loaf and I encouraged this new hobby as it was far better than when she went through her 'pickling era'.

I reached for a slice, but she pulled the plate back while smiling at me.

'Uh uh. You don't want to get buttery fingers on your new boots,' she said before popping the corner of a slice in her mouth.

Baz and I gave her our best puppy-dog eyes and she relented, handing the plate to me and tearing off a chunk for Baz.

'To be honest, Lois, I've mixed feelings about them,' I said, eying my boots with equal delight and annoyance. 'They're not something you'll find in most wardrobes, but I can't get over that price tag. It's still hurting to have parted with that much cash for them.'

Part of me was pleased to have an item that cemented the next stage in my mountaineering career, but I couldn't help but think of all the other things I could buy with £600. Since they are packed with insulation it costs a lot to make them light. They are a pretty niche item, so they are not widely manufactured, hence the eye-watering price tag.

'You never did tell me how much they cost,' Lois said, putting socks into my kit bag.

'What are numbers, really?'

'Ed, how much did they cost?'

'Less than our house.'

'Ed. How much did they cost?'

'Less than my . . . car.'

She turned and gave me that look that said she wasn't playing around.

'£600,' I responded in a low voice.

'What! You *could* have bought your first car with that!'

'I know, I know. But you can never really put a price tag on keeping all of your toes, can you?' Lois didn't respond, so I ventured, 'Thanks for helping, by the way. I'm a bit behind.'

'The quicker we can get this done, the better. The bedroom looks like a Go Outdoors store with a shortage of hangers. And I hope you didn't take that £600 out of the joint account.'

'No, no, of course not. I used your credit card instead.'

I gave her a grin and she couldn't help but smile back at me.

Peace restored and socks safely in the rucksack, I checked I had both pairs of the electrically heated gloves I needed. Everyone's hands get cold when they hit the minus temperatures of the peaks, but most people's don't curl into balls. These gloves might seem like a luxury item, but they would make the difference between me being able to hold on to my walking poles or not. Without the poles, I would be unable to stay upright on the mountains.

So much of my equipment had had to be adapted to help me get into the mountains. From loops being sewn onto my trousers so I could physically pull my left leg up, to the crampons that had been filed down so my left foot didn't get stuck on the ice, and the extra ventilation zips that helped with temperature regulation, as I can only sweat from the chest upwards, these adjustments made first hiking and then mountaineering a possibility for me. Now I wanted them to become available to others.

'This is new,' Lois said, eyeing up the extra zip in my trouser leg as she placed them into the rucksack.

I grinned at her, pleased she had noticed as I genuinely got excited about this stuff. 'They made an extra zip so I could get to my catheter bag more easily.'

My dream is to help accessibility become the new sustainability and move the whole industry in that direction. Accessibility is currently where sustainability was ten years ago and I want it to become essential, not just an occasional bonus. Berghaus had started doing this by adapting their kit specifically for different disabilities and I hoped that supporting them would encourage the other brands to follow. There were practical ways they could do this through the videos and photos they used, but it was also about the message they sent by championing accessibility.

'The zip was my idea,' I continued as we packed my clothes into the rucksack. 'Often, the adaptations are so simple but make such a huge difference. I might put a story on Instagram about it when I have finished this. It's part of the reality of different types of people getting up mountains. If we only see social media posts and adverts with fitness models or professional climbers doing it, it sends the message that hiking and mountaineering are only for them. But if they see people like me and Ben giving it a go, it will hopefully start to change that narrative.'

Lois smiled and gave me a nudge with her elbow. 'I'm glad Arron is going too. I always feel better when he's on these trips with you. He keeps you on the mountain, not falling down the side of it.'

That was undoubtedly true. Arron is an old friend of mine who is built like a tank and has helped me through, under and over some pretty precarious obstacles in the past.

'Could you pass me those two hiking poles, Lois? Actually, we'd better make it three.'

Lois raised an eyebrow. 'In case you lose one?'

'In case I break one.'

'They're supposed to be indestructible, aren't they?' she said, reading their tag.

'They keep saying they're indestructible, but I keep on managing to break them. I send them a photo of a bent pole each time I destroy one. Apparently, the German engineers see it as a challenge, so they keep sending me new and improved poles to test.'

Triple poles safely in my bag, I took the time to enjoy the quiet familiarity of us packing together, side-by-side. Every time I go away, I miss Lois after the initial excitement of the first few days wears off. We've been together since she was nineteen and I was twenty-one and it felt like we had grown into adults together. My accident changed the course of her life, too. She retrained as a life coach after what we went through and she also ended up founding a charity with me, which she also works for part-time. She has always supported me in my need to climb, never making me feel like I am being irresponsible, and even accompanied me on a few expeditions. That's the thing about Lois, she always encourages me with whatever new idea I have and doesn't hold me back or use my physical restrictions as a way of justifying me not trying things. It wouldn't even occur to her to approach it like that.

'Right, Baz. Sorry buddy, but we've packed everything else and it's time to shift you too. I need that jacket,' I said.

He raised his head but didn't budge, which wasn't like him. Lois waggled the last bit of sourdough at him, but he stayed put. Something was wrong if Baz wouldn't even move for food. Locked in a battle of wills, I eventually won by pulling the jacket out from under his solid four-stone weight.

Lois watched us quietly.

'Are you worried about the climb?' I asked, unsure of how to best broach this with her.

Lois and I didn't used to talk about our feelings, but we'd had to learn how to since my accident or we might never have made it through the event that changed both of our lives.

She looked up at me. 'Honestly, Ed, I don't like to think about it. But I've learnt over the years you always do what you set out to do. And you always come back safe.'

I leant over and kissed the top of her head with no doubt in my mind that I'd be back with her in just a few weeks.

CHAPTER 2

Namaste

'Are you ready?' I said to our videographer, Beetle, as we stood at the top of the travelator that would take us down into the arrivals area of Kathmandu airport.

Arron was standing further back and gave me a grin. He had visited Nepal before when we climbed Mera Peak together and knew what to expect once we crossed the threshold – pandemonium. Beetle nodded, wide-eyed with anticipation and straining to see over my shoulder.

We made our way down, each of us pushing our copious bags and a delivery of tents for Bigraj on several luggage trolleys. Few things can prepare you for Kathmandu airport at the start of the climbing season. As soon as our trolley wheels touched the end of the travelator, we were fair game.

I led the way as people swarmed around us, speaking to us in Nepali and offering to help us with our bags. I could see Bigraj pushing his way towards us through the crowd. I adjusted the course of my trolley and aimed for him.

'Wow, Bigraj has brought a lot of people with him. They're really helpful too,' Beetle said as someone plucked a bag from his trolley and walked beside him with it.

'Ed!' Bigraj exclaimed as he manoeuvred around a young

man who was deciding whether it was worth having a go at helping me with my heavy kit bag.

'*Namaste*, Bigraj!' I said, pushing my hands together in the prayer position and bowing my head – the very satisfying greeting they make in Nepal.

'*Namaste*, Ed,' Bigraj responded, mirroring me.

The formal greeting over, we went in for a bear hug. One of the trekking guides, Dil, put Buddhist flower chains made from orange marigolds around our necks to seal the welcoming ceremony.

'Right, shall we get moving?' I said to Bigraj as I tried to keep track of our luggage.

Bigraj smiled, said a few firm words in Nepali and handed out a few notes. The crowds dispersed, leaving us with just Bigraj and Dil.

'I thought they were with Bigraj?' Ben asked as we wheeled our trolleys towards the airport exit.

'It's the start of one of the main mountaineering seasons, so it's been a quiet few months work-wise for a lot of people here. They come down to the airport to help carry bags to make a few rupees.'

The double doors of the airport exit slid open and the warmth of Nepal's spring shone down on us, a nice change from the seemingly endless winter in the UK. Bigraj pointed towards the minibus he had arranged and we all piled in.

Settled in and buckled up, we drove towards Thamel, the narrow-laned climbing district of Kathmandu, which is heaving with restaurants, hostels and market stalls.

I stared out of the window as mopeds flew around our minibus, some of the passengers and drivers turning to wave at us. Lorries that would never get up the speed to overtake us still gave it a go and oncoming cars honked at them, only swerving out of the way at the last minute. Tuk-tuks carrying an extensive family of brothers, sisters, aunts and cousins, plus a few chickens for good measure, wobbled precariously around us, accelerators to the floor.

Beetle, who had never travelled to Asia before, gripped the headrest in front of us, a look of nervous exhilaration on his face, while Ben watched it all with calm interest. I suppose when you're an ex-paratrooper and have already survived a 1,000-foot static line jump where your parachute didn't open properly, there's not much that can faze you. There were no laws on Kathmandu's roads and if there were, they certainly weren't adhered to or enforced. Lanes meant nothing, piling the maximum number of passengers possible onto mopeds was clearly seen as a challenge and if you ever mentioned 'braking distance', you'd probably get laughed at. The crazy thing was that it generally worked. I'd driven around Nepal countless times and never seen an accident. Somehow, everyone seemed to miss each other by a few millimetres and then cheerfully carry on their way.

It wasn't long before we pulled up at my specially requested hotel. The Mulberry Hotel sat in the heart of Thamel, rose a proud seven floors – practically a skyscraper in Nepalese terms – and I knew exactly what was sitting at the top of that seventh floor. But it would have to wait as, right then, we needed a quick meal.

We bundled out of the minibus, mountains of bags at our feet. Coming from a Qatar Airlines A380 airliner, with its pristine seats, neatly packaged meals and churning air conditioning,

Kathmandu's chaotic dusty roads and the onslaught of layered smells of spices, sweat and unswept streets was a huge contrast. Everyone's attention was pulled in different directions. Arron was smiling up at the prayer flags stretched between each side of the street, a multicoloured reminder that despite Hinduism being the most practised religion here in Kathmandu, Nepal was still a secular state with Buddhism woven into many aspects of life. Beetle was eyeing the shops that opened late into the evening with their goods spilling onto the pavements, tempting Westerners to come inside, just for a moment, and take a look at their wares. Ben was gazing directly at the moon, perhaps trying momentarily to escape the neon lights and crowds pushing down the road, searching for the next place to stop and spend a few dollars.

My attention was focused on one thing: returning to my favourite restaurant in Kathmandu and sampling their momos, dim sum-like balls stuffed with mincemeat or veggies and served with various tasty sauces. Once our bags were safely inside the hotel foyer, Bigraj led the way. He had grown up in a remote mountain village but had moved his wife and child to Kathmandu a few years ago as it was essential for any trekking guide to live in the capital. This was the place where the tourists convened and the deals were done.

Kathmandu's streets were heaving and half the faces we saw were tourists heading to the mountains or returning from them. People came from all over the world to spend a few days trekking through the lower mountains or preparing to tackle one of the summits. Out of the melting pot of languages, I could pick out Japanese, Italian, Swedish and Hindi, interlaced with Aussie twangs and American drawls.

We wove through the streets, happily chatting between

ourselves as Bigraj strode ahead confidently. These were the streets that New Zealander Edmund Hillary had walked through in 1953 when he and the sherpa Tenzing Norgay became the first confirmed people to reach the top of Everest. After Edward Strutt and his team first tried to summit Everest in 1922 there were numerous other attempts, but none succeeded until Hillary and Norgay managed to make it to the top. These climbers of the nineteenth and early twentieth centuries were celebrities, the astronauts of their day. The amazing thing about Strutt's climb was that his team made it to 8,170 metres and it was just the last 700 metres that took a further thirty-one years to conquer. Mountaineering had such a rich 300-year history and I had been completely absorbed by it in recent years.

'Bigraj!' I shouted at his retreating figure.

He stopped and turned and I pointed to a bar I wanted to pop into. Smiling, he followed us inside.

'Take a look at the walls,' I said to Ben and Beetle while I bought them a beer.

Mouths open, they turned to soak up the hand-written notes documenting the decades of mountaineering history surrounding us. Beetle leant in closely and tried to read as many of the scribbled records as he could, his drink forgotten on our table. The Nepali-owned bar had started a tradition years ago that, on their return from the mountains, climbers would sign their names directly on the walls, along with the mountain they had attempted to climb and the height they got to. The walls were covered in these records, a testament to the greatest achievements of some of the climbers' lives. When I was last there, I had found a few notes that recorded climbing partners who had never made it back, their bodies laid to rest where they fell, rarely recovered due to either the impossibility of locating them or the danger to the rescuers. The walls also paid tribute to lost friends; grief that would follow the ones who survived for a lifetime.

Nepal is home to eight of the ten highest mountains in the world – including Everest, the highest at 8,849 metres – so it is one of the homelands of climbing. These walls also served as a reminder that the mountains of Nepal are about more than just Everest. Seasoned climbers knew that just because Everest is the highest, it didn't necessarily make her the most interesting. Instead, they came to Nepal to test themselves on some of the most technically challenging or dangerous mountains to summit, including Makalu and Annapurna, the latter having an alarming fatality rate of around a third of climbers. Himlung Himal, which we were heading to in a few days, was a much safer option. It still had its risks, though, and I had made a point of not telling Lois about the experienced Spanish guide who had sadly died on his descent after summiting in 2019.

That's the thing about climbing – when you are new to it, you become fixated on the risks on the way up, while most of the accidents actually occur on the way down after you have achieved your goal. You're exhausted and depleted and therefore more likely to make mistakes. Supplies are also more likely to be low. It's also a matter of simple physics. When walking, if you're going upwards, you fall into the mountainside and have more chance of stopping your descent. If you're walking downwards, you fall with the slope and gravity will try to take care of the rest. More experienced climbers are aware of the higher risks involved with the descent, but that doesn't prevent accidents from happening. Just look at what happened to Joe

Simpson and Simon Yates on Siula Grande in Peru in 1985. They were such skilled climbers they had managed to traverse the previously unclimbed West Face of Siula Grande and summit, but it was on the way down that things really started to go wrong for them. Simpson's book, *Touching the Void*, covered the harrowing events, where he fractured his leg. They tried to continue descending but fell into further problems where Yates had no option but to cut the rope tying them together – with Simpson at the other end.

Our beers finished, we headed to the restaurant Arron and I had visited the last time we were in Nepal, three years ago. When planning the trip with Bigraj, I was relieved to hear that it was still open. Many places had shut down during the Covid-19 pandemic, as international tourism had been heavily impacted and the Nepalese government had been forced to cancel all climbing expeditions. Mountain tourism is big business in Nepal and much of this was swept away in an incredibly tough year for all the porters, guides and tea houses that relied on this income.

The streets of Kathmandu were still busy even at this relatively late hour and Ben and I had to carefully manoeuvre around more than one group of celebrating climbers who might have had a bit too much to drink. Some of them hadn't even showered yet and the stench of unwashed clothes hung in the air long after they had passed. Stray dogs sniffed the streets looking for scraps and the dust rose and enveloped us every time a tuk-tuk sped by carrying passengers from one district to another. We turned down a tiny alleyway I remembered from our last trip and I hung back so I could catch the look on the boys' faces when they entered the restaurant.

Nestled in the dirty backstreets was an oasis of calm. We

were greeted at the front gate with the familiar *namastes* and the hostess turned to lead us with small steps through the mangrove trees that formed the restaurant's seating area. Lanterns hung from the branches, casting a soft light below and the fresh green leaves acted as a canopy, shielding us from the noise, dust and smells of Kathmandu. Here, we could taste the tranquillity of the Nepali countryside for a few hours while we ate until our bellies were full.

We each ordered quickly, keen to consume as many calories as possible in preparation for the 5,000 to 10,000 we would need each day on the climb. As we waited, Bigraj spread out a map where he had marked the route we would take, along with the places we would stay each night. It would take us over two weeks to reach the summit point of Himlung Himal. As usual, I hadn't chosen the quickest route for our expedition as I intended that we spend ten days exploring lesser-visited parts of the Nepalese countryside.

We each studied the annotated map closely. After a while, I lifted my gaze to Bigraj, who was staring at me expectantly.

'It looks like a great route, Bigraj. I asked for some remote exploration and you certainly delivered it.'

He smiled at me, his relief clear.

'This should give you a good intro to Nepal,' I said to Ben and Beetle. 'See there,' I continued, running my finger around a circular route. 'That's the Annapurna circuit, one of the most famous treks that takes you through the Annapurna sanctuary.'

Our food arrived and we carefully folded up the map to make room for the bowls that covered the entire table.

'Tell us about Himlung, Bigraj,' Ben asked, after the silence that often descends on a hungry table had passed.

His full, bushy beard made him already look like an experienced climber who didn't have the time or the mirrors for shaving and I had to keep reminding myself that this was all new to him.

'It is very remote and means Snowy Mountain. Not many Westerners there. You will get to see the real Nepal as it has been for centuries. It is not a very technical climb.' Bigraj raised his head from his bowl and smiled at me. 'It is a stepping stone. A great mountain to prepare for an 8,000-metre one.'

Bigraj knew all about my future plans for climbing. Since summiting Mera Peak, I had grown more interested in the technical side of climbing. In tandem with wanting to climb higher, I had also begun to learn about the art of climbing and I wanted something that would test a few of my new skills while also letting me reach the 7,000-metre mark without stretching my capabilities too far. It was indeed a stepping stone as I continued to push the boundaries of what a person with quadriplegia could achieve in these mountain ranges.

'An exciting stepping stone,' I added, returning his smile. 'What really appealed to me was how remote it is. I wanted to do an expedition where we are high up on the Tibet and Nepal border and wouldn't see any tourists for ten days. I like the idea of it being a proper adventure and heading off to lesser-trodden territory.'

'It is so remote we have to set up our own base camp,' Bigraj added, his pride in this clear.

That was why our luggage was so extensive. Not only had we brought over our own kit, but we had travelled with some of Bigraj's new branded supplies as well. It was going to be a journey of firsts for all of us.

Four years ago, Lois and I had stepped out of a taxi in the Annapurna region and approached a shy, smiling guide holding a sign with our names on it. Little did I know this trekking guide, who had limited English at the time, would become one of my closest mountaineering friends. As he led us on a three-day tour of the mountain villages where he grew up and worked as a porter, and as he took us up thousands of stone steps that linked the villages together, we got to know each other. He proved himself a highly capable and organized guide; he was clearly intelligent and motivated and always sunny and warm. He also managed to fish me out of a bush when I fell six feet off the side of the stone steps, so I knew he was calm in a crisis, too. Bigraj had worked his way up from porter to assistant trekking guide and then qualified as a trekking guide. He was respected by the people of all the tea houses he entered and everywhere we went, he was met by the locals with a huge smile. Bigraj quickly became mine and Lois's bridge to the Nepalese people.

All of that sealed the deal and Bigraj and I agreed to stay in touch. Over the weeks, we began chatting about climbing a mountain together and he recommended Mera Peak, as he had recently summited it and knew it would be accessible for me. When I returned a year later to climb Mera with fourteen friends, I asked the touring company for Bigraj to be allocated as our head guide. After summiting Mera and with another successful trip under our belt, I knew I had to do more to help him.

When I approached Bigraj about providing him with some funds to set up his own trekking and climbing company, he took some persuading but eventually agreed. However, he was adamant we should split all the profits between us. I was equally adamant that we wouldn't. It had always been clear to me that despite his considerable skillset, he was scraping a living, sending everything he earned back to his village in the Everest region to support his family, who he rarely saw. The last thing he needed was to send half his profits to me. I had done some digging and found out that the local guides and porters who worked for the big trekking and climbing companies, which were often owned by Westerners, hardly saw any of the profits filter down to them, even though they did all the work. That meant that even with the necessary ambition and skillset, they could never raise enough funds to set up themselves. It was an unjust and impenetrable glass ceiling.

After some persuasion, Bigraj agreed for me to help with the funds and a few friends assisted with the design and tech side. Bigraj then launched Ascent Adventures Nepal shortly before the Covid-19 pandemic. His ethos is to share more of the profits with the guides and porters, as he knows this money will filter its way back into the Nepalese communities. He had already trained up some of the porters and taken on the younger ones as apprentices. Despite the halt in tourism, Bigraj worked hard to continue establishing his business and taught himself fluent English in the space of a year.

'So, there won't be other groups staying with us at base camp then?' Beetle asked.

'Maybe,' Bigraj responded. 'But if we are the first we get to choose the location.'

It was going to be a proper adventure.

'I read that Everest Base Camp is like a small village,' Ben said.

Bigraj nodded. 'There might be 500 or even 1,000 people

there at the busy times. Lot of people doing the trek to Base Camp just to see it. 40,000 a year visit. Only a few hundred try to climb to the peak but depending on weather windows they can end up queuing to get to the summit.'

I leant back, finally full. 'Learning about high-altitude tourism has changed my whole view on it. I would still like to climb one of the 8,000-metre mountains one day. I'm just not sure if I could manage Everest.'

I had made this decision a while ago. For the moment, I just wanted to get better at mountaineering and had been trying out some technical rock climbing to help with that. It's challenging in a different way as it requires a variety of skills and techniques and isn't just about endurance.

'You'll be the first person with quadriplegia to get to 8,000 metres,' Ben said, smiling. 'And I'll be with you when we are the first to summit over 7,000 metres.'

'If we make it,' I responded. 'I was looking at some stats from the last year the government produced climbing records. In 2019, 122 people tried to summit Himlung and only fifty-two made it to the top. Come on,' I said as I pushed back my chair. 'I want to show you all something back at the hotel.'

Half an hour later, I pushed open the door to the seventh floor of our hotel. It was late and we were the only ones on the rooftop.

Beetle whooped when he saw what awaited us and ten minutes later, we all returned dressed in the appropriate gear.

Without waiting a moment, Beetle ran straight through the door and, with an ungraceful leap but with full marks for enthusiasm, he jumped into the small open-air infinity pool that was a rarity in Kathmandu hotels. I watched him with a smile, pleased he appreciated the very reason I had asked Bigraj to book this hotel for us. At $60 a night, Bigraj was flummoxed by the sheer excess of the expense, but after triple-confirming to him that I was sure it was what I wanted, he arranged it for us. Arron jumped in after Beetle while Ben and I were forced to take things a little slower.

Sitting on the pool's edge, I slowly slid my body down and enjoyed the feeling of the warm water holding me. On the rooftop, above the dust and mayhem, you could see all of Kathmandu's electric lights twinkling in the night sky to make up for the lack of visible stars. It might be a surprise that a person who nearly lost everything diving into a swimming pool would ever want to be near one again. But I never had a fear of water following my accident and even went back and swam in the pool that had tried its hardest to take me out.

I swam a few laps, pleased with the ease with which my body moved through the water. It supported me from every angle and gave me an agility I would probably never experience again outside of it. I glanced over at Ben. He was experiencing the same thing, too. Here in the water, we could both outswim Beetle and Arron; we were on a level playing field again. I leant back against the edge of the pool and let the water raise both of my legs towards the sky.

The next morning, before breakfast, I headed up to the roof terrace again. In the early morning light, I could see the faint grey backdrop of the mountains in the distance. They were calling to me, but I would have to wait another day before I could answer.

We convened at breakfast and then headed out into a muggy

day to get the last bits of gear we needed with Bigraj. Although his fluency in English had improved impressively from leading so many English-speaking groups since our climb three years ago (far better than my Nepali), the sentiment was still the same. We would risk losing a digit or two if we didn't have the right kit at -20 °C. Most people who are serious about climbing will bring most of their kit with them from previous expeditions, but there will always be the odd thing one of the climbing party will have forgotten or been unable to find. Beetle needed to rent some high-altitude boots and we were all happy to go along for the ride.

As we walked through the narrow streets coiled with tourists and shop owners trying to tempt them inside, I glanced down an alleyway and noticed a serene temple perched at the end. This was a common sight in Kathmandu and reminded me of how important religion is to the people who live there. We didn't have time to stop as Bigraj guided us to Shona's shop, the legendary Queen of Kit who we had first visited a few years ago.

The rental secure, we were soon wandering through the market stalls and I watched as Beetle happily snapped up around two suitcases' worth of cashmere, as he had already realized how much these goods were worth back in the UK. I hadn't known him for long – we'd only met once before our trip – but I had quickly realized that as well as being a brilliant videographer and talented sportsman, he was a proper wheeler-dealer. One who was interested in making a bit of extra money rather than trying to rip anyone off. He was doing our trip for expenses and experience, so good for him if he could make some extra cash on the side.

At 4 p.m., we arrived back at the hotel, hoping to get a quick swim in before heading out for an early dinner. Opening the door to the rooftop pool, towels in hand and swimming trunks on, we were met with an unusual sight. Covering the entire terrace next to the pool was some of the best high-end mountaineering kit I had ever seen. There were around forty items spread out neatly next to each other. Lying in the middle of it all on his back was a Middle Eastern guy in his mid-thirties. I looked up and saw his friend leaning over the balcony overlooking the rooftop pool, taking snaps of him chilling on his back with all his mountaineering gear surrounding him. It was a classic 'pic for the 'gram' moment.

I wandered over to take a look at his impressive kit.

'Where are you heading out to?' I asked as I bent down to admire the latest Black Diamond head torch.

'I'm going to climb Everest. I head out tomorrow.'

'Amazing!' I stared at everything spread out on the ground, pleased to meet an experienced mountaineer. But something wasn't quite right.

'All your kit is brand new. Did your luggage get lost at the airport?'

'Oh no. I just bought it all in Kathmandu when I got here.'

'But where's all *your* kit?'

He looked at me like I was a bit slow. 'This *is* my kit.'

Then it dawned on me. He hadn't been to the high mountains before and he was about to take on the highest of them all.

'Oh, right,' I responded.

I honestly couldn't think of what else to say as he seemed so excited by his 'adventure'.

This is the problem with mountaineering at the moment. Someone who had never put on climbing boots before was about to tackle the world's highest summit. He would have paid a minimum of $50,000 for the trip and partway through it he would inevitably have to turn around. The unscrupulous climbing company wouldn't care that he wasn't fit enough or experienced enough to attempt the climb because they'd already been paid. Most climbing companies wouldn't have taken him on, but some of them don't care about the risk to the climber, guides and porters. Not to mention the mountaineers who have to negotiate a peak filled with inexperienced climbers.

You can't just go and 'climb Mount Everest'. You have to build your way up to it by experiencing different climbs and working out whether you can learn the skills needed and how you react to the altitude. Making it to Everest Base Camp is a feat in itself, as it sits at 5,364 metres – one of the best technical climbers I know can't go above 5,000 metres as his body just shuts down. Then, to get up from Base Camp to Camp 1 on Everest, you have to traverse the Khumbu Icefall. And, yes, it's as dangerous as it sounds. It's a glacier that moves about a metre every day with crevasses so wide you have to walk over ladders that have been strapped together, wearing your crampons. You're told just to stare at your feet and try not to look at the yawning drop into the stomach of the mountain hundreds of metres below you. It is insanely dangerous, like most 8,000-metre peaks, and that's just the first leg of the journey.

He had no idea what he was in for and I silently hoped he wouldn't find that out in the most tragic way.

CHAPTER 3

The Battle of Besisahar

It was 'only' 5.30 a.m. when we made it to the hotel lobby and were met by big grins and warm handshakes. Bigraj had been joined by our trekking guides, Dil and Rabin, as well as a few porters who would be helping us on the expedition. Once the pleasantries were exchanged and we had received our orange flower chains, we loaded up the cars and left Kathmandu for the mountains. A couple of days was always enough for me in Nepal's capital and I longed to explore the countryside. But before we could test our trekking legs, we had a twelve-hour drive to get through.

Our final destination of the day was Danaque village in the Annapurna sanctuary, which was so rural it didn't even appear on Google Maps when I'd looked it up the previous night. After six hours of bumpy, potholed driving, we stopped to grab lunch in Besisahar and received what I can only describe as an enthusiastic welcome from the local kids. Holi, or the colour festival, is a national holiday in Nepal that celebrates spring's arrival and the triumph of good over evil. As far as I could tell, this meant people took the day off work and threw paint at each other, which I always wholly endorse.

As we stumbled out of the cars, legs cramped from six hours of sitting, we emerged into a showdown that had clearly been playing out for hours. There was an enormous friendly street fight between the local kids, all armed with paint-filled balloons. The ones at street level were being hammered by a clever few who had positioned themselves belly-down on the rooftops. Once the street-level kids spotted that we newcomers were well over six foot tall, we were immediately recruited as we could almost reach the paint-balloon snipers. I looked around for our translator, Bigraj, but he had headed off for a cup of tea. So, through a series of huddled strategy meetings, which involved a lot of pointing at the roofs, we devised our attack plan and the kids loaded us up with balloons. The watercolour-paint-filled balloons soared high and soon our adversaries on the roofs had gracefully admitted defeat. It made me think about whether this would ever happen in the UK. Children at home don't really play in the streets anymore and even if they do, they are so alert to the stranger danger they would never try to pull us into their game.

Liberally splattered in paint and with Ben now sporting a green beard, we spent another six hours on bumpy roads, driving past emerald-green rice fields before arriving in the small village of Danaque. At 2,400 metres high, we were already around double the height of any mountains the UK had to offer and we hadn't even walked a step. It was dark when we arrived, so we found our tea house, had a quick meal and bunked down for the night. Five days of trekking through the Himalayas lay ahead of us before reaching our base camp, where we would begin the long process of the crucial acclimatization hikes. This was just the beginning of our journey.

*

The light filtered through the tea house window behind my bed at 6 a.m. Reaching behind me, I pulled back the curtain and stared up at the snow-capped peaks before me. The trip had properly begun.

Arron held an introductory qigong session and the guides and porters were encouraged to join in, and even the expedition cook, Kumar, was willing to give it a go. Have you ever been in a park and seen a group of people doing what looks like slow-motion karate? They were probably doing qigong (pronounced 'cheegong') or possibly t'ai chi. They are closely related and both hail from China. As well as being a personal trainer and gym owner, Arron is a qigong instructor who has studied Chinese medicine and Eastern wellness practices for over ten years. Qigong is a moving meditation that works with your inner energy, known as qi, to help you keep healthy and fit and to aid longevity. I was a bit sceptical when I first came across it as I was so used to the high-impact, adrenaline-fuelled training I had known in rugby. My rugby career had raised me to believe in 'no pain, no gain'; the harder we train, the better the results. So, I went into the practice feeling restless and wondering what it was really doing. But like most things, with a little effort, I got a massive amount out of it.

Following this, we enjoyed a traditional breakfast of chapati, chilli and eggs to fuel our first day on foot. Our primary job of the morning was to re-pack our bags so the crew of porters could balance out their considerable weight before setting off ahead of us. We had already sorted through our luggage in Kathmandu and left everything we wouldn't need in the mountains, such as jeans and T-shirts, at our hotel, as we had to keep the weight of our luggage close to 10 kg. Our morning task was to decide what we would carry in our small backpacks for the day's hike, such as food and water. The porters would walk ahead of us with our larger rucksacks packed with clothes and other items.

It's funny how the amount you carry on a hike changes depending on the different climbing level you reach. If you were heading out for a day's hike in the UK, you would carry what we had in our bags that day in Danaque – some food and water, perhaps a few plasters and baby wipes. The stage up from this in the UK is when you're hiking for two or three days and must carry all of your kit, including a tent, sleeping bag and stove. I had done this several times on fundraising walks throughout the UK and knew how tiring it was to carry all this essential kit with you. Then, when you travel to the Himalayas and hike and climb for three weeks, you go back to carrying just a small backpack again, as you have porters to help out.

Even an elite climber will use porters to get to the base of the mountains as it's a way of supporting the local communities. If they are proving themself with an unassisted climb, the 'unassisted' part usually only starts from base camp. On our last trip to Mera Peak, one of the participants had insisted on carrying his full rucksack – much to the dismay of his porter, who was worried he wouldn't have a job for the next two weeks. This guy was super fit, but the extra weight increased his susceptibility to altitude sickness. Unused to the heights we were climbing to, he was one of the first to bow out of the summit day. If we didn't have porters to carry our luggage, Ben and I would never have been able to access these places. They would be closed off to us, with heavy rucksacks threatening to tip us over because of our shaky undercarriages and also increasing our risk of altitude sickness. The porters made the mountains accessible to us. Even without spinal injuries, the vast majority of trekkers and climbers in Nepal rely heavily on porters because of the negative effects of altitude such as breathlessness, headaches, fatigue and sleeplessness, which are all increased by carrying heavy luggage. They needed people to help them, and this is where the concept of porters stepped in.

Our primary packing job done, we all went outside for a team photo with the porters and guides. Dil and a young trekking guide, Pasang, would join the porters that day, helping with their loads, while Bigraj and Rabin would be our guides. Each porter balanced their load, consisting of two of our bags tied together with a strap, against the wall and leant forward with part of the strap around their forehead. It was only then they could stand. The muscles the porters have developed in certain areas of their bodies, and their strength to carry the backpacks, were incredible. With a wave, they set off up the mountain as if we'd just given them a toothbrush to carry. They always left before the hikers or climbers as they wanted to go at their own pace. It was more comfortable for them and they didn't want to hang around as we gawped at the beautiful landscape like the tourists we were.

We were keen to walk around Danaque village before we left, but with just a few rock-strewn pathways, there wasn't far to explore. Despite the continuous rain, all the boys and men wore flip-flops and the women smiled at us from small porches as we passed. As tourists, we weren't a rare sight – Danaque relies on farming and passing trekkers for income. It is a regular stop on the famous Annapurna Circuit, which loops around the mountain range and takes two-and-a-half weeks to complete.

It was our plan to travel the circuit for a day before peeling off for a more adventurous route.

We returned to our tea house where a week ago our donkeys would have stood in the same small field, each numbered one to eighteen. They would have rested for the night, just as we had done, before carrying on with their journey to the site of our base camp with all the tents, climbing equipment and gas canisters. We had to take all of that infrastructure with us because Himlung was so remote. They were several days ahead of us now and Bigraj had told us we would soon meet them on their way down.

I knew the contrast in tea houses would be dramatic as we continued our trek. In Danaque, we were in relative luxury, sharing a bedroom with only one other person, and there had even been pizza on the menu the previous night. Later in our trip, I knew we would all sleep in much more rustic accommodation.

When Bigraj gathered us together to start our day's hike, it was as if a small starter gun had been set off. Rabin nimbly led the way up the steep climb out of the village. We were always bookended by guides to ensure no one got lost, with Rabin always at the front and Bigraj at the back. If we had been a larger group, there would have been another guide in the middle with us as well.

It didn't take long for the thinner air to become apparent and we soon all settled into a regular pace we could each match. Trekking at these altitudes works your body harder as there is less oxygen in the air, so we were all breathing deeply to try and compensate. Still, everyone was making good time as we followed the winding pathways formed from centuries of use.

I got into the steady rhythm of trekking uphill, pleased to finally test my body in the altitude again. High clifftops surrounded us and loose stones were scattered across all of the pathways. Some of these stones were contending for the title of 'large rock', so my gaze had to stay firmly on my feet while moving so there were no trips or falls. I changed from a biped to a quadruped in the mountains, as all four of my limbs accounted for my mobility. My walking poles weren't just there to steady me, they dug into the pathway and gave me the leverage required to move my weaker left leg forward – they provided me with four-wheel drive.

A couple of hours passed and every now and then, I would stop to admire the river hundreds of metres below or gaze up at the distant mountains. The sheer vastness, the colossal scale of those ancient formations, always reminded me of how small I was and, consequently, how minute my problems were. I have always enjoyed the perspective they released within me and as we walked, I reflected on how happy I was to be back in Nepal again.

When I arrived in the mountains, I had switched from my electronic ankle foot orthotic (AFO) to my manual one. My accident had left me with a foot drop on my left side, which might sound like a relatively minor inconvenience but it is the reason I can't lift my left foot. The only thing I can do without an orthotic is swing my leg around in a large circle if I have a walking pole or stick to lean on. That was never going to work for more than a few steps on flat tarmac, let alone on these off-piste treks, so I had learnt how to walk with an AFO early on in my recovery.

Over the years, I had tested many of them and found one

made by TurboMed that fitted outside my shoe. Most AFOs go inside the shoe and sit underneath the foot, which caused enormous problems for me. If you've got something very solid in your shoe, bunking up with your foot, it's going to rub. And if you can't feel when things are rubbing, you're likely to end the day's hike with less foot than you started with. Not an ideal outcome. The TurboMed AFOs also allowed my foot to drop all the way to the floor on the way downhill, so I wasn't just walking on my heel with less grip. As Nepal isn't exactly known for its flat terrain and half my walking would be downhill, this was pretty essential. Ben also wore an AFO, but his foot drop was on his other leg so together we had a matching pair of orthotics.

By the middle of the morning, Ben pulled up next to me and we dropped into a steady pace. I had been thinking about how he had been getting on, so was pleased to see him.

'How are your pain levels today?' I asked after we had walked in silence for a bit, both keeping a careful eye on where we were placing our feet.

'Pretty average,' he responded. 'I took my meds a few hours ago. They've kicked in, so I should be set until we get to Koto.'

I knew Ben was probably being stoical due to his background as a paratrooper with the British Army Parachute Regiment. Physically, Ben was more capable than me and walked with a much smoother gait, but he had ongoing chronic pain from nerve damage.

Beetle had finished his filming for the morning, so he began to walk with us, too. Our skilled photographer always had a bounce in his step, even on the mountains, and while he bobbed along, I swung my left leg up with much less ease.

The sun was now high up in the sky and there was less shade to relieve us of its fierce rays. The temperature was soaring and, for once, it wasn't just me pouring with sweat. I also noticed that Beetle's pale Scottish skin was gently cooking due to a lack of sunscreen. We slowed to a more enjoyable pace in the midday sun while Beetle and Ben got to know each other.

'Ed told me you were in the paratroopers,' Beetle said. 'My dad was in the army as well.'

'Thirteen years,' Ben replied, smiling. 'The last couple of years were in a rehabilitation hospital. Joined when I was 17 and left at 30.'

'Ben was a personal trainer in the regiment,' I added. 'That's why I thought he could manage this trip with us, as you can't get much fitter than that.'

'You're certainly having no problems keeping up,' Beetle said. 'But you're a lot quieter than the army PTs my dad told me about.'

Without warning, Ben hollered, 'Press-up position! Lower, raise, lower, raise! On your feet! Too slow. Back down!'

We all jumped. I'd never heard Ben raise his voice above conversational level, now he was shouting like a disgruntled lance corporal.

Ben grinned at us. 'I was a different person in the army. It's only after leaving it that I became quieter. I had to be that shouty, angry person, so maybe it was a facade that I got moulded into. The people I used to coach and train told me years later that I was ridiculously fit but a *horrible* PT.'

'What did you do?' Beetle asked.

'The normal stuff we had to. We'd go out for a nice steady run, but then someone would annoy me, so I'd increase the pace. They'd try and keep up with me and I'd think, "So, you reckon you're fit, eh?" So, I'd increase the pace again. Then I'd shout, "Press-up position!" and they'd drop and do press-ups. We'd keep on running and I'd increase the pace again. People would vomit at the end of it. But they got fitter.'

It reminded me of some of the more brutal rugby training sessions I'd put myself through.

Ben explained that being a PT was only part of his job and that his primary role in the army was operating Gun No.1. This meant he was the sergeant in charge of a light gun called an L118. The term 'light' in the army shows the scale of their weaponry as this gun weighed close to two tonnes. It was more like a cannon. He had a detachment of six men he was in charge of, including a bombardier, a lance bombardier and usually four gunners. His detachment's job was to look after and operate the 'light' gun.

'I don't understand,' I said, interested in this behind-the-scenes intro to the paratroopers. 'I thought a paratrooper's job was to jump behind enemy lines.'

Ben smiled, his eyes lighting up. 'That's a widespread mis-conception about the paratroopers. It's not so much about the "behind enemy lines" side. The parachute regiments were formed because it was the quickest way to deploy a mass amount of troops. If you think about it, it's usually too dangerous to land an aircraft close to the enemy, so they parachute everyone out and all the equipment they need.'

'So, they parachute out the gun?' I asked, trying to imagine how they safely got a two-tonne gun out of the back of an aircraft.

'And a vehicle as well.'

Now I was imagining jeeps being lobbed out of the back of flying aircraft too.

Ben caught the look of alarm on my face. 'The gun and vehicle are stripped and boxed up on a multi-stress platform at an angle, so they don't get damaged in the drop. It goes first, with two parachutes attached, and we jump afterwards. Then, it's our job to locate it and put it back together. Once we have attached the gun to the vehicle, we are a mobile unit awaiting our orders. Fortunately, I've never had to do it in battle, as it's a pretty high-level combat situation requiring that type of specialist deployment. But our job in this situation would be to support the infantry in front of us, as we could fire up to 17.2 kilometres ahead of them.'

'Bloody hell,' I said, stopping to grab some water from my bag and passing the sunscreen I had found to Beetle. The heat in the narrow canyon was becoming overwhelming. 'I didn't know guns could even fire that far.'

'Me neither,' Ben said. 'Until the army took me on.'

We all fell silent for a bit.

'Even though my main job was looking after my detachment, it was good I had the personal training side to my work,' Ben continued, taking out his own water bottle. 'I think it helped with my recovery after my accident.'

'My surgeon told me my fitness levels helped me survive,' I said. 'I bet yours did, too. A 1,000-foot fall is not something many people would get through.'

The circumstances of both mine and Ben's accidents were a question of odds. The chance of these accidents happening in the first place was one in thousands, but the odds of us surviving them were also very slim. We could view ourselves as unlucky to have had them happen to us or lucky to have survived. Which viewpoint you spent most of your time pondering would largely dictate your experience of your recovery and sometimes even the outcome.

'I had a chat with my surgeon about it,' Ben said, as he set off again. 'I had been thinking about how I managed to survive. He said it was my fitness, determination and training, but one of the main things was I wasn't aware I was falling. I thought my parachute had opened up.'

'Couldn't you see it hadn't?' asked Beetle, his face now shining from a liberal application of much-needed sunscreen.

'I'd done my checks to see whether it was open, but because I hadn't jumped for a couple of years, I didn't have a visual comparison of how big it should be. It hadn't deployed properly, although it looked like it had. When I glanced at the ground to help assess which way the wind was blowing, the ground was literally *there*. I didn't have time to brace or tense up, which is when the damage is done. When you're loose and floppy, the impact isn't as hard. My surgeon told me that's why drunk drivers usually survive horrific crashes, as they don't even know they're happening. I landed standing up but didn't even break my legs. The shock of the impact travelled up them and my L2 vertebrae burst. It took the brunt of the fall.'

'Is that the same place as yours, Ed?' Beetle asked.

I shook my head and stopped so I could steady myself to point to the base of my neck. 'I dislocated my C6 and C7 vertebrae and it was the disc in between that burst.'

'The L2 vertebrae is lower down on the spine,' Ben said, pointing to an area a couple of inches above the waistline of his shorts.

When people with spinal cord injuries discuss their recoveries, you will often hear them drop in a T10, L3 or C4. These letter and number combinations might not mean much to most people, but they give us a quick idea of the extent of the other person's injuries. Each is the location of a vertebra and follows a logical order down your back: C1-7 run down the neck, T1-12 are the upper and mid back and L1-5 cover the lower back. The location of the damage to the spinal cord is critical as everything below it will be impacted, while everything above will usually be less affected. This is why I had issues with curled hands that Ben didn't have, as the nerves that ran out to his arms were well above his injury site.

'We both had shards of spinal cord that meant there would have been no chance of us walking again if they had moved a millimetre,' said Ben. 'The payback for that is we both lost sensation and the ability to feel pain in one of our legs.'

'Here's to the millimetre club,' I said to Ben, holding my hand up for a high-five.

It's incredible how a few millimetres can make the difference between whether you would walk again or not, or even life and death.

Ahead of us, the path curved and we all stopped in our tracks. In the distance was the eighth-highest mountain in the world, Manaslu, standing proudly by itself. It was first summited by a Japanese team in 1956, three years after Edmund Hillary and Tenzing Norgay successfully tackled Everest. At 8,163 metres and with its sharp serrated edge of a peak, Manaslu had captured my attention for the past year and I had wanted to see it ever since. The reason it intrigued me is that it's one of the more accessible 8,000-metre mountains because it doesn't have any technical sections and can be approached from three different sides. I wondered if it would be accessible to me.

A couple of hours later we arrived in Koto, where we would stay for the night. It was a colourful Wild West-type town in the shadow of Annapurna II and would be our last opportunity for connectivity to the outside world.

Strolling through the only main road, we quickly realized that when it came to paint shades for the houses, anything went in Koto. Pink for the first-floor walls and turquoise for the second? Not a problem. Red for the window shutters and bright green for the balcony struts? Don't hold back! It worked beautifully – an expression of the freedom and joy the people of these mountains embodied.

The next day we would be heading off-grid for the remainder of the expedition, when we would peel off the main trail and head towards Himlung Himal. I checked myself over and was pleased to see there were no holes in my feet. Ben had told us about an ulcer on his foot that his doctor in the UK had told him to keep an eye on. He had told us it was doing well, and it didn't seem to be holding him back. I was faring well, as was the rest of the team, thanks to us being a relatively fit bunch.

At our tea house, we tucked into a big meal of egg noodles with potentially too much homemade chilli sauce. I knew I might regret the double serving of sauce the following day, but I decided to let future Ed deal with that. It was still warm, so we decided that instead of braving a mad dash to the outhouse shower later, consisting of cold water in a bucket with holes, we would go down to the river for a quick dip instead. With our towels stashed on the riverbank, we went all in and plunged into the meltwater stream, followed by a quick scrub to get the visible dirt off. It wasn't the most comfortable wash in the world, but it definitely woke us up. We quickly dried ourselves and I treated myself to a fresh set of clothes before returning for our final meal of the day. As we sat around our table, I could feel everyone's nervous excitement as we waited for our food. The following day, we would leave the main trail and strike off on our own.

CHAPTER 4

Donkeys Don't Wear Crampons

The previous day's four-hour walk was a pleasurable Sunday jaunt to a local pub compared to what we would face on our second day of trekking. We had a nine-hour trek ahead of us up a remote valley towards Tibet and by the end of the day we would be 1,000 vertical metres higher than where we started. Before I got into this type of trekking and climbing, I hadn't really grasped the concept of vertical metres and what that meant. Look out of your window and try to imagine you are over a kilometre higher in the sky – that was where we would be walking towards from Koto.

Before we left, we knew it was our last chance to send a message to our loved ones. As soon as we struck off the Annapurna circuit, we'd lose Wi-Fi and signal and our mobile phones would function solely as cameras and calculators (or possibly projectiles to wake up our tent mates if they overslept). The evening before, I had sent Lois a message telling her I loved her, I'd be okay and in contact soon. The lack of communication would be difficult for us both. Usually, we dash off messages to each other as most couples do, but I knew this one needed some thought as we would be off grid for so long, so I spent some time tapping it out. We were carrying a satellite phone, but that was just for emergencies, not general chitchat or catch-ups. The whole point of the trip was to disconnect from the outside world so we could enjoy the benefits of being fully present in our surroundings and this meant messages and calls only in an emergency.

I wanted to record a video for Instagram as well, as I knew it would be a while before I could thank people who had donated to the charity Ben was raising money for. At the end of the recording, I said, 'Someone asked me the other day if I was scared of death. And I read an amazing quote and it stuck with me, "I'm not scared of death. I'm just scared of not living."' For me, the entire expedition was living. Trekking and climbing in the Nepalese mountains were something I never thought I would be able to do even before my accident, let alone after it, and I wanted people to see that no matter what happens we can achieve more than we think we can.

With our goodbyes sent into the ether and strong coffee drunk, we set off from the village towards what looked like a gorge fit for Jurassic Park. As we wound up the steep-sided valley, it was hard to concentrate on where we were putting our feet. At every turn was a vista that would quite literally take our breath away. Cliffs shot upwards, world-famous peaks appeared when least expected and 200-foot ribbon waterfalls plummeted to the streams below. The vegetation was lush and green, with pine trees hugging the banks of the river. The sound of tumbling, churning water accompanied us everywhere and added to the majesty of our surroundings. I glanced around at the group and their grins conveyed equal pleasure in these sights. It was as if Beetle was inside a pinball game as he raced ahead, then darted behind, trying to capture everything. At one point, I caught up with him and he was a ball of energy with two cameras in his hands and his head swizzling from side to side. 'There are just too many epic shots to choose from!' he declared.

Breathtaking views soon gave way to a breathless hike up a path covered in loose shale that was angled at forty-five degrees and shot up the side of the valley. Gaining altitude quickly and on an uneven terrain, I struggled to draw in the oxygen I needed and things quickly began to get a bit dicey.

Placing the tip of my walking pole into the pathway, I felt it lose its purchase. *Shit*. I was going to fall. I tried to swing my left leg up quickly enough to steady myself, but it wouldn't respond in time. The world tipped and the familiar feeling of not being in control hit me. I curled my body in, protected my neck and let my arm take the brunt of the impact. In only a moment, Arron was by my side, had checked with a quick thumbs-up that I was okay and was helping me back to my feet. I dusted myself down as Beetle tried not to stare at me, unsure what to do as he wasn't yet used to my tumbles.

'I'm fine,' I said and I honestly was. That one hadn't hurt much and I reasoned it would only result in a cracking bruise the next day.

Beetle nodded and carried on ahead to catch up with Rabin. He hadn't made a fuss, which was how I liked it.

'I'll stick with you on this stretch,' Arron said. He had such a calming voice that just speaking with him put you in a Zen-like state.

Arron was used to my tumbles, just as Bigraj was. Ben had experienced his own in his recovery, so he didn't flinch at mine. Even if Arron hadn't been used to them, I had never seen him stressed. 'Flap' is not in his vocabulary. He just checked I was okay, got me back to my feet and, for the rest of the steep pathway, caught me twice when my wobbly footing threatened to throw me to the ground again.

Falls had been part of my daily life when I was learning how to walk after my accident. They became the norm, but I had never got used to the distress they could cause to some people who witnessed them. I had learnt how to minimize the damage as I went down in the early months after leaving hospital, but I had never learnt how to placate onlookers quickly. If they panicked, there was little reassurance I could immediately give them other than hopping up and doing a comedy jig – which I couldn't do anyway at the best of times. I was relieved to finally know that all my teammates wouldn't freak out if I fell in the coming weeks.

I'd taken a punt when I had asked Beetle along, but the signs he should join us on this trip were too strong to ignore. When our videographer dropped out two weeks before we were due to depart, I was worried we would struggle to find a replacement. Finding a decent videographer for a couple of days is hard enough with only two weeks' notice, let alone someone who could drop everything and fly out to Nepal for three weeks. Unsure of what to do, I put a story on Instagram explaining I needed a last-minute replacement and crossed my fingers. A day later, there were fifty applicants, which surprised me as we were offering expenses rather than a fee. But then, it was an appealing trip providing unique footage to add to their portfolio.

As I sorted through the applicants, I realized a few chancers wanted a free trip and could barely use an iPhone camera by the look of their pages. There were also quite a few well-meaning but inexperienced people and some who had missed that it was expenses only and had sent over their eye-watering day rates.

But as I sifted through, there were five who were young, keen, fit and, most importantly, hugely talented. Sitting on a train back from Sunderland, I called the first one and explained I would need to meet him if we would be sharing every waking hour together for three weeks.

'Totally understand,' Beetle responded. 'My signal is dropping but I'll give you a call to arrange to meet up when I get off my train to King's Cross.'

'Um . . . wait a second,' I said. 'I'm on a train to King's Cross. Which one are you on?'

It turned out we were both on the same train. Beetle was coming back from his parents' house in Scotland, but it was a route I rarely took. If it had been Bath to Paddington – a train I got all the time – it would have been less of a coincidence. It seemed that fate was giving me a rather large nudge. So, we met at King's Cross and had a beer. Beetle was ginger, Scottish, loved life, was ridiculously fit and up for a challenge. Sold. The only worry was he'd never been tested at altitude and might have one of those physiological make-ups that can't hack it, but we'd just have to give it a go. The signs were too strong to ignore. Now it was clear I had been right to follow them.

The steep path we were traversing mercifully gave way to a gentler slope as we were all panting from the reduction of oxygen. All of us apart from Bigraj and Rabin, that was. They had grown up in these altitudes. This was effectively their sea level and I wondered what sort of endurance feats they could tackle if they ever visited me six metres above sea level in Somerset. They would probably be completing Iron Mans before their morning Weetabix.

While I took a break to admire the scenery, I quickly checked my phone to see if Lois had been able to respond to my message before we left. With a groan, I realized it hadn't been sent. The message I had carefully crafted the previous night hadn't even left my phone. Crap. Lois wouldn't know I was thinking about her and to top it off, she would see a post on Instagram and wonder why I had time to share a lengthy video, but not a few lines for her. I had spoken to her a couple of days before but knew I might be in the doghouse for this one. I also knew she would be updating my mum back in the UK who always worried when I was away on these sorts of trips.

My worries briefly lifted when, half an hour later, we were all excited to cross our first patches of snow.

Ben stopped when he spotted it and shouted behind to Bigraj, 'Do we need crampons?'

This was met with Bigraj's biggest grin as he responded, 'Donkeys cross this. Donkeys don't wear crampons!'

To be fair, he wasn't wrong.

Ben smiled and shrugged, as everything Bigraj said was delivered with good humour. The path levelled out and Arron dropped behind to chat with Bigraj about the settlement we would arrive at the next day. Phu village is known for its deep spiritualism – as is Arron, so his eagerness to reach it was understandable.

'I've been meaning to say thank you,' Ben said as we walked, 'for bringing me out here. I know it wasn't easy to get the insurance and that it nearly didn't happen because of that.'

I thought of the call I'd had with Ben where I had told him we would fund his trip to climb Himlung Himal. He had burst into tears, his response confirming how much it meant to him.

'Don't worry about it,' I said. 'It's never easy to get insurance if you've had any sort of medical condition. I'm just pleased you decided to come.'

I saw a lot of myself in Ben, starting with his determination to walk again after a spinal injury when the odds were against him. There are also many similarities between professional rugby and the armed forces. The larger-than-usual proportion of burly blokes aside, they're both all-encompassing careers where people join young, forge their identities and have a team that becomes a family. When you leave – or occasionally get spat out the other side – many people end up asking, what's left? You're sitting at home by yourself, without your team, and you can find yourself in limbo very quickly. That was where Ben had found himself. He was floundering without a purpose. When I first went to Nepal in 2019, it changed my outlook on life. Because Ben was in such a similar position, I was hopeful he would have the same experience.

'Do you miss rugby?' Ben asked after a while.

Not many people have asked me that. Maybe they see it as intrusive or insensitive and perhaps something that reminds me of better times. Ben knew it was just a normal question to ask and far preferable to always sticking to the 'post-accident' side of my life.

'I miss certain elements of it for sure,' I said after thinking for a moment. 'The electricity in the tunnel as you line up next to a team you're about to go to war with, waiting to run out in front of thousands of people . . . that's hard to replace. I also miss some of the locker-room antics and that I don't see as much of my teammates these days. But to be honest, I don't miss playing and training that much. I did it for ten years and I'd already had seven operations when I retired at twenty-eight.'

I grinned at him. 'I'd started preparing to leave well before my accident as I only had a few years left. I think if the accident had happened when I was twenty-one, there would have been more "what ifs" regarding my career. It would have probably been a lot more difficult to deal with, but having had the opportunity to play for ten years, I can look back knowing I had a proper stab at it.'

'I didn't have a clue it was coming,' Ben said as he pulled ahead of me. The path had narrowed and we could no longer walk side-by-side. 'I'd finally found somewhere I belonged after years of bullying at school and being told I'd amount to nothing. But I'd shown them. I was a paratrooper in the armed forces. I had brothers there. And then, *bam*. One routine parachute jump and it was all taken away. I lost my job, home, the use of my legs and my purpose.'

'Wave for us,' Beetle shouted from way up ahead, halfway across a rope bridge that spanned a deep gorge.

We both dutifully waved to the camera and I wondered if Ben's smile reached his eyes.

Beetle gave us the thumbs-up before dropping behind to capture Arron and Bigraj walking together on the bridge.

'I still can't believe it happened,' Ben continued when we had both successfully traversed the wooden slats that were the only thing between us and a drop of a hundred metres into the river below. 'I mean, I never expected to stay in the armed forces forever, but I thought I had another ten or twenty years left. I was so fit, Ed.'

His voice cracked and he turned away from me.

I had spent many a night trying to convince Lois that Ben should join me on the trip. As Ben's life coach and the CEO of Millimetres 2 Mountains, Lois knew he needed a goal and a purpose, but she wasn't sure whether one of the charity's beneficiaries should come on a trip that was quite so extreme. The other trips we took beneficiaries on often required stamina, but there weren't usually any peak climbs or summiting involved. But I had pushed back and told her I was confident Ben was ready. I had pretty much guaranteed it. Physically, he was much more capable than me and I knew he would get so much out of the trip. We were taking a chance with Ben, but it could be pivotal as he had to make a new path.

I glanced at him, unsure if I should try to reassure him or change the subject. 'There's no doubt you were thrown a curveball. But you're doing everything to hit it out of the park.'

Ben brightened. 'That's why I wanted to do this climb with you. I *will* get to the top of this mountain and prove people wrong.' He turned to me, his eyes shining. 'People think we're not capable of summiting a peak like Himlung, but I'm going to show them what we can do.'

My stomach dropped. I had guaranteed Ben was ready for this climb, and physically, he clearly was, but I hadn't realized how much he had tied up in it emotionally. The mountains don't work that way. You can be the most determined and technically proficient mountaineer in the world and not summit on any given day. All you can hope for is to come back in one piece – and even that can't always be guaranteed. It's too much to expect that your ability alone will deliver the day's outcome. There is so much more to it than that.

*

57

Eight hours after we set off, we entered a small forest with bark and spent pine needles coating the ground. The hush it brought to our world, away from the continuous gushing of streams and waterfalls and the crunching of our boots on gravelled pathways, was noticeable. The air smelt of fresh pine and, no longer in the sun, the drop in temperature was pronounced. It was beautiful and we all needed the peace it brought to get through the last hour of our day's work. That one kilometre of vertical metres had equated to twenty kilometres of high-altitude trekking and pain was creeping in.

I don't often talk about pain. It's not a word I like to spend much time on. While I'm in the midst of these challenges, I'm reframing my thoughts to look for the positive and I'm also very forward-thinking. That's why I keep taking endurance tests. When I look back at them, I almost immediately forget all the difficult bits and times of struggle. Then in the middle of the next challenge, I think, 'Oh God, why am I doing this again?' This was the exact thought that popped into my head in the last hour of our trek that day. It was the first tough session and, consequently, the first time I realized this mission we had set ourselves was going to be a difficult one. Until this point, it had been quite gradual, but with the combination of the altitude and the terrain on the second day, it had quickly become pretty tough. There was definite pain shooting through my body. More than usual.

Since my accident, I have constant pain in my knee from an old rugby injury where most of my meniscus was removed at the age of twenty-three, so it is now bone rubbing on bone. In my twenties, I'd also had three operations on my shoulders that always flare up as soon as I start using my walking poles.

There was also pain caused by my accident, as my quads and hamstrings on my left leg don't work properly to brace my knee. That's the thing about injuries that layer on top of others. My accident completely changed my gait and where the pressure runs through my body. Muscles and tendons have to accommodate others that don't work as well, bringing on new problems or exacerbating old ones.

I was incredibly lucky that rugby gave me the fitness levels to help me survive my cardiac arrests in the back of the ambulance. But it also gave me a body that had been operated on multiple times, torn, fractured and degenerated well beyond my twenty-eight years. If you speak to any rugby player after an entire career or on reaching their fifties, they all have knee or hip replacements. Parts of their bodies have degenerated to a level like someone in their eighties might experience – and it's not as if they get paid that much to do this to themselves, in comparison with other sports. But you never consider that at the time. You're just happy to be there and paid to do something you love every day. It's all you've ever known.

All day we had been walking in the foothills of a mountain, sometimes literally underneath it with tonnes of stone hanging overhead when the pathway cut into its side. In the late afternoon, as we trekked through another valley, Rabin pointed out Meta village up ahead. Behind it was one of the smaller mountains in this range. Kang Guru dominated the skyline even though it was a couple of hundred metres smaller than Himlung Himal.

Up ahead, there was a colourful monastery perched on the side of a scrubland hill with Meta village nestled underneath it. Our first glimpse of where we could finally rest spurred us on through the last few kilometres. We arrived after nine hours of trekking at a fairytale village, perched on a plateau surrounded by giant peaks. As I watched the eagles circle overhead, the pain I was feeling momentarily drifted away.

That evening, I laid out a set of clothes I had warmed by the fire on my bed and then made my way to the outhouse shower. I stripped down, mentally shored myself up and pulled the handle that released a spray of icy water. After quickly dashing some soap around me, I grabbed my towel, teeth chattering, and scampered back as fast as I could to my warm clothes. Even inside the tea house, it was cold enough to see my breath and it felt as though I would never get warm again. The higher we got, the chillier the shower water and the air we emerged into after we cleaned ourselves. Long gone were the refreshing tepid showers in the jungle region.

Later, as I huddled by the fire in our tea house and waited for my food, I thought about how much that day had already demanded from my body. It was a reminder of how beautiful yet savage the Himalayas can be for someone who can't walk 'real good'. We were now definitely into it and I knew Arron would be worth his considerable weight in gold by keeping my questionable rig in some sort of working order.

CHAPTER 5

The Village at the End of the World

I woke up on a wooden board that had served as my bed for the night. The boys were still fast asleep on their respective planks, which lined the walls of our room, giving me the time needed to get my body moving. Even at home, on my plush mattress and six metres above sea level, I can't hop out of bed and begin my day. Overnight, my body stiffens because I barely move while asleep. When we sleep, we automatically adjust our position when it becomes uncomfortable, but I don't have that degree of movement, so everything locks up. I tend to wake up in the same position I fell asleep in, with a pillow still clamped between my knees to try and stop my back from being put out. This lack of subtle nocturnal adjustments means my body needs longer to fire up.

This process began with rolling off my side. Pain shot through my hips and lower back, my body demanding that I lie quietly and let the day slip by. But my mind knew better. I had learnt in the early months of my recovery that half an hour of stretches would usually bring back my full mobility. If I remained in bed as my body always pleaded, it would be even harder to move the following day and the battle between my will and body would be further stacked in the latter's favour. This would continue until my muscles began to atrophy and the precious movement below my neck, which I had fought so hard for, slowly slipped away. That wasn't an option, so I always got moving in the morning, no matter how awful I felt.

As I lay in bed, I gently rolled my ankles and wrists before gingerly urging my quads and hamstrings to play their part. I think if most people woke up feeling like I did, they would call an ambulance; it really is that bad. Pain sparks in so many directions that you would think I'd been in a car crash.

Once I felt there was a chance of being able to walk, I pushed myself into a seated position, biting the inside of my cheek as I tried not to yelp at the burning sensation flaring out from my knee. My body whispered, 'Just lie down for a bit longer. It's better that way.' But I knew from experience the pain I felt didn't always warn of further damage and wasn't always a sign to stop. This type of soreness had to be broken through, so after a few minutes, I slowly fitted my orthotic and pushed myself to my feet. A spasm shot down my left leg and I landed with a thump back on the board. Thankfully, my sleeping bag broke my fall. Spasms don't take me by surprise anymore and when one hits, as they invariably do in the mornings, they usually send me crashing to the ground, my leg buckling beneath me.

'Sorry,' I said as the others looked over, bleary-eyed. 'Just trying to get going.'

'No worries,' Beetle mumbled before rubbing his face to wake himself up.

Always ready for the day, Aaron unzipped his sleeping bag and was on his feet in a minute. 'I'm going to get us all some tea. See you at the front for qigong in half an hour?'

'Definitely,' I responded, as I tried to push myself up again.

Another spasm hit and I toppled down to the plank once more, this time missing my sleeping bag and wincing as pain shot through my coccyx.

'Don't mind me, I'm just getting through my morning break-dancing routine.'

Arron grinned, as he'd travelled with me enough times to know he couldn't assist in this and I just needed to let the spasms run their course. He also had a far better way to help: qigong. As well as helping my body wake up in the morning, it also aided my mental health as there is a great deal of mindfulness to it. Since arriving in Nepal, we had also been doing it in the evenings and it helped us wind down for sleep with slower movements and the focus on breathwork. But in the morning, Arron led us in sessions that fired up the body and got the blood moving.

Once I got to my feet, Beetle was already dressed and heading out the door. I leant against the wall and started a series of stretches that began to lessen my pain.

'You go ahead,' I said to Ben, who had patiently waited for me for the last five minutes.

Ben nodded and, with his orthotic already in place, went to meet the others. I stared longingly at the door, wanting to explore the village we would soon be leaving, but I knew I wasn't ready yet.

Ten minutes later, I had managed to hobble down the corridor to empty my night catheter bag and change it to my day one. Once I had brought all the equipment back to my rucksack, I walked back to our room door, my gait still not having smoothed out. A spasm shot down my leg, but I was too quick for it. I grabbed the window ledge and put my weight on my other leg. 'Won't get me this time,' I said aloud as I waited for the electricity passing through my nerves to settle.

With a smile from my small victory, I went into the corridor. I opened up the wooden door to our hut and paused. I had forgotten about the ladder.

The previous night, it seemed quite exotic to scale a fifteen-rung ladder to reach our sleeping quarters. That morning, as I stared at the drop in front of me, 'exotic' was not the word I would use. 'Potentially expedition-ending' would be a more appropriate phrase. I turned around and slid my body downwards, so my stronger right foot found its first rung. My hands tried to curl around the ladder's sides, but they weren't fully working yet and their grip was loose. Next foot down, I felt a bit more confident. One more and I even craned my neck around to try to see where everyone had gathered for the lesson. That was when the spasm hit. The leg with all my weight on it buckled and my body dropped. Scrambling to grip the ladder, my hands slowed my fall somewhat but my shoulders were wrenched. I landed in a heap at the bottom of the ladder.

I knew the score. I carefully checked myself over, paying careful attention to the places where I couldn't feel pain, and all seemed well. My pride was more bruised than anything and I hoped no one had seen my fall. I knew one day my luck wouldn't hold. But it had once again and that's all I could really ask for.

I pushed myself to my feet and headed past the grazing donkeys to the edge of the front lawn where Arron had found a mound to conduct his lesson. Our group, including the porters and guides, had already gathered and Arron indicated I should join Bigraj at the front. Always putting his students first, Arron had his back to the otherworldly valley we'd ascended the day before. In the distance, the golden morning sun emphasized the towering Annapurna range and Arron's backdrop was so mesmerizing it was difficult to concentrate on his instructions.

We started with a few simple movements, pushing our hands outwards to adjust our energy. Immediately, I began to relax. Next to me, Bigraj was entirely in the zone, placing his feet exactly where Arron instructed, his movements careful and precise. This was how Bigraj approached everything, with an open mind and an innate enthusiasm. He constantly wanted to learn. When we walked together on these treks, Bigraj would always quiz me about our way of life in the UK, as he is interested in other cultures and how things work. In among his English, he now scattered phrases he had picked up from us, such as, 'It's cool, man' or 'How's it going?' He's driven by wanting to provide a good life for his family and community and knew learning about Western culture would help him understand his clients better and how to meet their needs.

Arron has a similarly inquisitive mind and that was partly why he became an instructor in qigong. He had been a personal trainer for years when he came across the practice and decided to learn more, as he was interested in helping his clients on a deeper level with their physical and mental health and not just training them to look good. He once told me he slips a bit of qigong into most of his client training sessions, whether they know it or not, as he wants to help with their energy and stress levels so they can heal from the inside out.

I glanced behind me and could see Dil gawping up at the sky. When he clocked me watching him, a serene look settled on his face and he joined in again. I smiled to myself. It was like being back at school with the distracted kids at the back. The qigong session had clearly not landed with everyone, but you only got out of it what you put in.

Qigong and chapati omelette sandwich done, we set off behind Rabin, Bigraj's sidekick. Unfortunately, my gag to Bigraj about this making him Batman was met with confusion. Apparently, I had found the only corner of the globe that hadn't heard of Gotham's finest.

A couple of kilometres out of Meta, in the very far distance was our first glimpse of the snowy mountain range of Himlung Himal. It was exciting to finally see it after planning this trip for over a year, but my first thought was, 'Bloody hell, that's pretty far away'. I put my head down and continued to hike ever upward as there was still a vast distance to cover to get to the base of our mountain.

As we followed the Phu Valley, it was clear we were now crossing into a more remote part of Nepal. The landscape was starker, with grassland a dried-out brown colour rather than the fresh green of our earlier days. But the subdued colouring only provided more contrast to the brilliant, crisp whiteness of the snowy peaks that now surrounded us. The locals we encountered were shorter and the otherworldliness of our location was further emphasized when we stopped for lunch in a tiny village where all the houses, even though they were inhabited, didn't have roofs. If you've ever seen *Star Wars*, it felt as if we were in Tatooine and I was half-expecting a pod racer to whizz past. If you haven't seen *Star Wars*, please accept my apologies for the unknown reference. (And then go and watch *Star Wars*.)

For lunch, we had dal baht, Nepal's national dish. It consists of lentil curry (dal) and rice (baht). These are usually served in separate containers with perhaps a small bowl of pickles to accompany them. It's filling and an excellent option to pick in the tea houses as you will usually be served seconds. With the more Western-style dishes, there is a one-portion maximum and you'll only receive a few tuts from the grandma matriarch who runs the show if you dare to ask for more. The higher you go, the more dal baht dominates the menu until you reach somewhere as remote as Phu Valley, where there is no menu. It's just dal baht. When I first met Bigraj, I was surprised to hear he has pretty much eaten dal baht three times a day since he was born. As I said, it is firmly the national dish of Nepal.

As with all of the establishments we visited on this trip, our food was served with care and many smiles. Bigraj had told us the tea houses along the route were incredibly grateful to have guests as there weren't many tourists who travelled to these places and we were the first team they had seen for a long time. For this particular meal, we were pleased when our dal baht arrived with a lovely bit of yak meat. Now I know some veggies out there might be pondering how we could have tucked into a shaggy fringed bovine who helped out in the mountains by transporting goods between villages. What had a yak ever done to us? Well, tell that to the snow leopard that killed it two days earlier. Yep, that's right. We were so remote our lunch was served up via snow leopard. If that's not ethical meat-eating, please let me know what is.

After lunch, we followed the valley upwards, clinging to Indiana Jones-esque pathways cut into the side of cliffs hundreds of feet above the charging river below. Four hours later, high on the hills above, we saw the telltale colours of a Buddhist gate, which was the entrance to our destination. We were now at 4,000 metres above sea level and the steep climb to the gate was a shock to the lungs. But it was worth the effort once we saw the fluttering prayer flags of the village at the end of the world: Phu.

In just a few hours, the landscape had changed so dramatically that there were no longer any trees and the ground was largely barren soil and scatterings of rocks. The vegetation was sparse, with only the occasional scrub bush dotting the hillsides. As I headed for the white gate with colourful flags on top that marked the village's most apparent boundary, I was transfixed by the homes in the distance. In most of the villages we had passed, the buildings were spaced out, but here in Phu the stone houses were terraced in places and stacked on top of each other as they followed the line of the mountain. Stone slab pavements weaved between them, with the stone houses blending perfectly with the mountainside soil. The only colour was the prayer flags and the occasional painted roof or window ledge. I had never seen anything like it.

Phu is known as the most remote village in Nepal and is more Tibetan in its culture and style. To give you an idea of how isolated it is, the Nepalese government only discovered its existence thirty years ago when an official noticed an unmapped settlement out of a helicopter window. Its inhabitants had been living there in almost complete isolation for hundreds of years. No one was aware of its existence apart from Tibetan traders to the north and monks who travelled to the monastery.

Ben and I passed through the white arch with 'Welcome' on either side and I immediately turned to him. 'Did you feel that?'

'Yes,' he replied. 'I've never felt anything like it.'

There had been a sudden shift in energy when we walked

through the archway and I instinctively knew this was a place of deep spirituality. Never before had I felt such a tangible sense of a higher power in the air. The prayer flags caught my attention once more and we all stood and watched them for a few minutes. There was no need to hustle through the village, chattering loudly. We just wanted to rest in that moment and watch the squares of coloured material flutter in the breeze. My only wish was that Lois was there to witness it.

When we were ready to move again, Bigraj led the way and we all quietly followed. The village was eerily deserted and Bigraj explained that most of the inhabitants migrated to the lower cities of Kathmandu or Pokhara during the winters and hadn't yet returned. Even for these hearty people, the harsh winters could be too much. There was, however, a core of residents who remained through the bleak, snow-filled winters to tend to their yak and it was one of these shepherds Bigraj was trying to find. Phu sat in the rain shadow of the giant Manaslu and Annapurna ranges, resulting in little annual rainfall and a desert-like environment compared to the jungles of the Everest region. Little grew up there, but somehow, the people of Phu had made it work for centuries and have relied on their livestock to help with this. Not only that, they had created a truly stunning settlement with very few resources and relied heavily on their livestock.

We followed Bigraj through the narrow, winding pathways, sometimes with five-foot stone walls on either side, and ducked through low doorways where I whacked my head a few times. Eventually, we found an elderly man who informed Bigraj there was only one guest house open, which had been filled by another team heading for Himlung. Unfazed by this news, Bigraj had a few more probing conversations with other residents and we were soon welcomed into someone's home for the night. Our expedition cook, Kumar, got straight to work in the kitchen, assisted by Rabin and Dil, while our host found some blankets for the thin mattresses upstairs. That was how it seemed to work over there. There was never any awkwardness, even among strangers; everyone just mucked in and helped out in whatever way they could. There were definite benefits to a society where everyone had to pull their weight and there was no time for laziness or egos. Our two trekking guides helped Kumar without pulling rank or needing to be cajoled into it. Instead, they all just came together to do what needed to be done and everyone was happier for it.

Evening fell and we sat around the fire in the kitchen while Bigraj and the boys busied themselves cooking dal baht. A single bulb hooked up to a car battery and a solar panel on the roof lit the low-ceilinged stone room. The electrical cables didn't make it as far as Phu, so the residents had to be completely self-sufficient. I leant back and surveyed my surroundings. The warm glow of the fire flickered over the owner's family photos – they had all travelled to the lowlands for the winter while he remained to look after their yaks.

We sat on the floor together, ate dal baht and laughed at jokes most of us didn't understand. It was about as authentic as it gets and I could feel that even the porters who spoke no English were enjoying our company, as we were theirs.

The following morning, we did our daily qigong session before discussing what to do with our day. We would spend two nights in Phu to acclimatize, as we were now above 4,000 metres and moving higher too soon would put us at risk of altitude sickness. After the two days of hiking we'd had, staying put was welcomed and we were in no rush to move on.

Phu monastery was calling to all of us, so we immediately headed up a winding path towards it.

'Do you think we'll get to meet a monk?' Arron said. 'I hope they are back now.'

I didn't respond as he had already asked this question several times and we wouldn't know until we arrived. Like many of the villagers, the monks also left Phu during the winter months, but their destination was Kathmandu, where they spent their time studying. They were due to return imminently and Arron was frothing in anticipation of meeting one. I also wanted to meet a monk, but I was a bit worried that Arron might faint if one happened to have arrived the previous night.

I had visited monasteries in Nepal before, but this was a new experience for Beetle and Ben. The main monastery building was locked, but we peered through the windows and saw a large room where every surface had been painted a different primary colour. The ceiling was blue, the pillars red and the gauze curtains were yellow. Red and gold flags hung from the ceiling. The place was so still. The person showing us around informed us that the monks hadn't yet returned; Arron's disappointment was palpable. After a while, we went outside, which was just as beautiful, with thousands of prayer flags, painted rocks and *stupas* – small colourful monuments containing relics – flowing across the hillside. Monks or no monks, the monastery was incredible.

We spent the next few hours just 'being' and time slipped by as I sat next to Arron. We had first met when we were both around twenty, on a night out with mutual friends. I was sporting peroxide blond hair, which I thought was pretty edgy, and he was growing sideburns that didn't last very long. We were young, out for fun, and the city of Bath was our playground. Over the years we bumped into each other on many a night out and always shared a couple of beers, but it wasn't until after my accident that we became close. I had heard about his training that had other 'elements' to it. Intrigued, I booked a few sessions and quickly realized this wasn't just about throwing weights around like I was used to. There was a deeper layer to Arron's work and I attribute my recovery, in part, to Arron's sterling input. We spent more time training together and something just clicked, so I started inviting him to come on my adventures with me. If you'd told those two young men who spent their weekends bombing around the bars of Bath that in fifteen years' time, they'd both be sitting on a flat rock, quietly filling a few hours by staring at some colourful flags, they probably would have both spat out their beers (and then ordered another round). But that's what time, experience and a life-changing accident have done to me. And I'm better for it . . . although I still appreciate a round of beers.

I wasn't in any way spiritual before my accident. A career in rugby doesn't provide much opportunity or tolerance for anything otherworldly. It was during my initial days in hospital, lying in bed at night trying to get my head around the possibility of a lifetime in a wheelchair, that I became more interested in the mind-body connection. In the early months, it had more to do with the power of a positive mindset and what that helps you overcome and the opportunities it opens up. That is all rooted in science as well – the mind's state really does physically manifest in the body. But over the following years, there were too many 'coincidences' and nudges, such as opportunities arising just when I needed them, to ignore. I can't say exactly what I believe, but I suppose that's kind of the point of spirituality – it doesn't demand a full commitment from us. All I can say is I believe there is something bigger going on. It might all be explained by science in five hundred years, but I just know there is something more than the day-to-day. Entering the gate of Phu the day before had been another instance of this, as we all felt a change in energy. These occurrences made me consider whether there were certain fields of energy humans didn't understand because they couldn't identify or measure them – yet.

I closed my eyes and listened – silence. It had been a few days since we had disconnected from the outside world and, despite the fatigue, I relished a sense of calm and space in my mind that I hadn't experienced for a long time. It's not until you completely disconnect that you recognize the cloud of stimulus that we live our lives under. Sitting there without distractions, just the warmth of the sun on my face and the cool breeze on the back of my neck, I felt completely present and utterly calm. I could sometimes get to this place back home through walking, meditation or mindfulness, but it doesn't last like it did in the mountains. It was just a shame I had to go to such lengths to experience it.

No one had spoken for at least half an hour when Arron said, 'Have you noticed how the voice inside your head has disappeared?'

I already had as I'd been in this position before, but Beetle looked shocked as the realization of this dawned on him, while Ben smiled and nodded. The constant whirring voice we all have nattering away inside our minds had subsided and left some space behind for us to be still and appreciate the present moment. Everyone is different, but it usually took me around three days of disconnection with the outside world to clear the fog. There was no anticipation of emails to answer, jobs to do or people to call. It was just you and your mind in that moment. I looked up from the rock I was sitting on to see that Arron's moment had become qigong among the prayer flags and Beetle's was trying not to make a mess of the monastery thanks to a dodgy tummy. Everyone's moment was different.

On our return, we spent a leisurely afternoon napping. It wasn't long before we were back around the fire laughing at each other's terrible jokes, whether we understood the language they were delivered in or not, and looking forward to the climb to base camp the following day.

CHAPTER 6

Bigraj's Base Camp

I wasn't sure why I had woken so early the following morning. There was no need to be up when it was still pitch-black outside. Perhaps it was the anticipation of travelling to the foot of the mountain I had been dreaming about for two years. Knowing I wouldn't fall asleep again, I deliberated about what to do as it wasn't my house to roam around. It was a relief when I heard muffled voices downstairs and knew I wasn't the only one awake. Without any electricity upstairs, I put my head torch on, rolled off my thin mattress and fumbled around for my shoes. I went through my usual stretches until my body was moving again before making my way downstairs as quietly as a drunk baby elephant.

Smoke was gently seeping from under the kitchen door and I ducked down to enter, having hit my head on that particular doorframe several times already. Bigraj and Rabin's wide grins greeted me and we exchanged *namastes*. Rabin wrapped a cloth around the metal handle of the giant teapot that hung over the fire, which was the natural hub of the room for heat and food. We were above the tree line so the locals burned yak dung for fuel, which didn't smell anywhere near as bad as you might imagine. Rabin then poured me a glass of masala tea, which I gratefully received in the cold of the pre-dawn light. It was amazing what a smile and a cup of melted sugar could do for me in the morning. We had already christened Rabin 'Honey Monster' for the amount of sugar he put in any drink he served us. The nickname had struck a chord with one of our trekking guides, Dil, who had already replaced Rabin's name with Honey Monster and would tell everyone we passed about it.

It may have only been 5 a.m., but I couldn't have been happier to be out of bed. As we sipped our tea in the sparse stone room, the rest of the crew began to roll in, including two new faces I hadn't seen before. With an air of unbridled confidence, they wore their caps backwards and La Sportiva approach shoes on their feet. They were taller and leaner than the rest of our party and I immediately knew these were our two climbing guides for Himlung Himal. Bigraj introduced us to Pemba, who liked to go by the nickname of Shyam, and Kaji. We all shook hands.

Climbing guides tended to remain in the peaks during the two mountaineering seasons in Nepal, because they don't want to waste precious time trekking down to the lowlands. Instead, they travelled from base camp to base camp. It also helped them stay acclimatized if their base level is around 4,000 metres or higher. That was why they had found us in Phu rather than Kathmandu.

If we were in an American high school, climbing guides would be the quarterbacks. In Nepal, there is pretty much no more prestigious job and you'll see many of them rocking around the slopes with aviators on and spare carabiners jangling on their belts. They have every right to be proud of their work. It's an incredibly challenging and dangerous job and difficult to qualify for – many of them would have worked their way up from porters at fourteen years old. They could jangle away as far as I was concerned. They had earned it.

Bigraj explained that Shyam and Kaji were close friends who often guided together, but they had different specialities, which was why he had chosen them to head up our ascent. Shyam was interested in the lure of 8,000-metre mountains and was working his way through them. He had summited Annapurna, with its toe-curling fatality rate of around a third of climbers, twice. He was aiming to be a climbing guide on Everest in the next couple of years, which was technically much easier than some of the mountains he had already summited. But he knew that he had to summit the highest mountain because many of his clients would expect that on his CV.

Kaji, who was older and a little quieter than Shyam, was more interested in perfecting 6,000- and 7,000-metre mountains and had been a climbing guide for nearly fifteen years. He had summited Himlung Himal many times and would be the lead guide on our trip. Some of these 'smaller' mountains were far more technically challenging than many of the 8,000-metre ones and for him, size didn't matter; it was the skill involved.

It was immediately apparent we were in safe hands. Compared to what Shyam and Kaji had already achieved, Himlung Himal would be a doddle – exactly the position you want your climbing guides to be in. If things go wrong at 7,000 metres, you don't want the person you turn to for help to be on Struggle Street himself.

The crew was complete, so after we scoffed down Bigraj's signature breakfast (thick pancakes with melted protein bars on top), we set off from Phu and headed towards base camp. The path headed steeply out of the village, curling around what

I would call a mountain but Bigraj described as a hill: 'If there is no snow on top, there is no mountain.'

My body felt ready, but as we headed higher and the air thinned, trying to grab a breath while moving uphill was proving increasingly difficult. Rocks and boulders littered the uneven path and I had to stop several times to pull my left leg forward for its next step. Minimum hip flexor and no hamstring activation made stepping over things very difficult and, combined with a brain struggling to concentrate because of fatigue and less oxygen, a few stumbles ensued. Fortunately, Arron was by my side and quickly prevented any of the larger falls from happening. I could feel the climbing guides' eyes on me and felt a bit like a show pooch failing to perform. Despite all of this, we were making good time and it was great to see the other boys, especially Ben, moving so well. Apart from Beetle's dodgy stomach and susceptibility to sunburn with his ginger hair and freckled translucent skin (did I mention he was Scottish?), he hadn't had any adverse effects from the altitude. At over 4,500 metres, everyone looked surprisingly fresh and my hopes were high.

After a particularly tricky stretch, I glanced at our two new guides behind me. There was a look of confusion or perhaps concern on their faces, which quickly changed to big smiles. I wasn't surprised at their reaction; it's a look I am used to out in the mountains and it would be a bit strange if they weren't concerned about what they had got themselves into. Climbing guides are responsible for their clients' safety and if things get tricky high up on the mountains, lives can be in danger – yours *and* theirs.

Stopping for a moment, I pulled out my water bottle and

they passed me by, their grins still wide and genuine. Bigraj, who always remained with the last person, hung back with me.

'Do they know about mine and Ben's situations?' I asked Bigraj when I was ready to start walking again.

He smiled at me. 'Yes, I tell them, "He don't look very strong, but he is very, very strong".'

Now I had my new social-media bio sorted, I pressed on.

'When I booked them, I told them you've climbed Mera Peak, so they are okay,' Bigraj continued.

When they signed up, the fact that I had summited Mera Peak at 6,476 metres must have been pretty comforting for them. But now they had seen me walk, I wondered if they thought I had either paid Bigraj to say that or had one of his family members held hostage. Feeling the pressure to dig in and keep up the pace to set their minds at ease, I left Bigraj gathering up the rear of our party and overtook Ben and Beetle with Arron by my side.

Soon, I found myself teetering on the edge of a place that I lovingly refer to as 'The Bin'. Most people won't have experienced this, but it's when you push yourself so far in fitness or conditioning that it feels like every cell in your body is screaming, but you're still continuing as hard as you can. Your vision narrows, your lungs are burning, you're breathing heavily and there is a metallic taste from the lactic acid in your mouth. If you're at altitude, you can chuck in some dizziness for good measure. Fortunately, I was able to hold it together and avoid falling entirely in, which would have been quite embarrassing before we had even reached base camp.

After three hours of trekking through an increasingly barren landscape that bordered on volcanic in its bleakness, we met with our first full view of the Himlung range and Himlung

Himal itself. All of us stopped to take her in, only our panting breath breaking the silence. As I traced my gaze upwards, her rock-strewn sides whipped up into soft peaks with the most defined summit point I had ever seen at the crown. I was transfixed. She was beautiful. The photos hadn't done her justice, but they rarely do.

With only an hour to go until we arrived at base camp, I decided to spend some time with Ben. I regularly walk with the beneficiaries of Millimetres 2 Mountains, both in the UK and further afield, and while doing so, I like to ask them coaching questions I'd worked on with Lois. I've found that the scenery helps them open up in ways they might not when sitting in an office or on a video call with me.

After we had chatted for a while, I asked Ben, 'What are the three things you're most proud of?'

He thought about it and responded, 'Getting into the paratrooper regiment. And walking for the first time after my accident.'

'Both very fine achievements,' I commented.

'And the third one is summiting Himlung Himal.'

I tried not to react, but putting so much pressure on a climb and elevating it to one of the greatest achievements of your life when you hadn't yet done it was a pretty dangerous psychology. Many climbers suffer from 'summit fever' when they get close to the top, an incredibly risky state. The type of person naturally drawn to climbing mountains is often very goal-orientated and used to achieving what they set out to do. I recognized this in myself and Ben and this meant we had a predilection for summit fever – a state where we would be so fixated on summiting that we would ignore any signs indicating we should be turning around. Driven by a desire to reach the top, people with summit fever put their lives in danger because, with oxygen-depleted minds, they could not properly assess their situation and took risks they wouldn't have done further down the mountain. They forgot about the energy reserves they would require to descend and expended everything to get to the top. I had read about so many deaths, particularly on Everest, where climbers ignored the advice of their guides and had literally been half-dragged to the top, only to completely collapse as soon as they turned around. I was beginning to face up to the uncomfortable realization that Lois might have been right and that I shouldn't have pushed so hard for Ben to join us.

'You know there's a lot between us and the top of that peak,' I said to Ben, pointing towards its crisp pinnacle with my walking pole.

'I know, but I'm also absolutely certain we can do it.'

'I think that in perfect conditions, we can. But it's not just a case of mind over matter. We can't just reach the top and get down safely through sheer determination. It doesn't work like that out here.'

'Oh, so how does it work?'

'Before we set off from base camp, the guides and porters will all say a prayer to the mountain, which they call a *Puja*, because they believe it's the mountain's decision whether we get to the top or not. I feel that way too. Even if you don't believe the mountains work that way, we all have to understand there are so many things outside our control, such as the weather and snow conditions. If the mountain doesn't want to be climbed, it's not going to happen. It's not solely a case of willpower and effort.'

I didn't add that, given our circumstances – our medical

conditions and experience – the odds were actually against us summiting.

'I can understand where you're coming from,' Ben said, after some thought. 'But I'm going to bring everything I've got to this. I'm not going to hold us back.'

'I never thought you would,' I said. 'Just remember that the summit is just half the journey. We've got to get down again as well.'

It might not have made my top three but watching Bigraj show us around his base camp was definitely one of the top ten proudest moments of my life.

A couple of hours before we reached base camp, Bigraj had gone ahead of us. When I arrived with the boys, he was standing proudly among the ten or so tents his team had set up. There was also a large communal tent and an equal-sized kitchen tent for us all to gather in. Their positioning looked well thought out and I couldn't wait to explore. Our base camp was at the foot of the mountain, spread across an area the size of a football pitch that consisted of hard brown soil and scatterings of rocks. The snow crept down the mountains to the edges but did not cross over. As I raised my gaze to the sky, I realized life had been simplified to three colours: brown, white and blue.

'Welcome to the base camp!' Bigraj said, as I walked towards him and we hugged. He then went around and greeted everyone in the same way. 'I'm so emotional!' he proclaimed, spreading his arms out to indicate everything he had built through years of hard work.

He wasn't the only one who was feeling emotional.

'I'm so proud of you,' I said, as I followed Bigraj on the tour of our camp that would be our home for the next week. Everyone had been waiting for our arrival and reaction to their work.

I followed Bigraj as he excitedly showed me around. While he did this, I tried to imagine him as a fourteen-year-old porter who had to leave school to support his family and wondered what that Bigraj would say about all of this.

'Look here,' Bigraj said, pulling me over to one of the many bright orange tents positioned closely together. 'Nice one, eh?'

I watched as he rubbed his hand over the logo emblazoned on the tent with 'Ascent Adventure Nepal' written underneath. It was official. Bigraj had his own trekking and climbing company that was all his and no one could take it from him.

Beetle was filming the special moment and said, 'Whose is that? Who owns that?'

With two thumbs-up and the biggest grin, Bigraj turned to the camera and said, 'It's Bigraj's. And Ed Jackson's!'

Without warning, tears began to roll down my cheeks and I turned away from them both and began quickly wiping my eyes in the hope no one would see. But of course, Beetle had spotted this – he would have been a pretty rubbish videographer if he hadn't. He came over, still recording, and asked how I was feeling.

I turned around and said with a smile, 'I'm feeling a bit emotional.'

Not one to leave a pivotal moment unearthed, Beetle continued with, 'What's going through your head?'

'I'm just happy,' I responded, trying to get a grip on my tears, which were now being documented. 'I'm happy for Bigraj. He works so hard and he deserves all of this so much. It's so good to see it all coming together. I've known him for a long time and it was a dream back in 2019. Now it's here. I'm just happy for him.'

I stepped away using my walking poles to ensure I didn't take a tumble in front of the camera and announced loudly, 'It's the altitude. That's why I'm crying. Nothing to do with any of this.'

Beetle laughed and we wrapped up the filming session as I headed towards the dining tent to look at what Bigraj's hard work had created.

The following morning, I woke up having not exactly slept like a baby. I never do in tents, as it's pretty tricky to stay hooked up to a catheter bag and be zipped inside a sleeping bag at the same time. Combined with a firm surface and spasms, it produced a pretty restless night. Even so, it felt amazing to unzip my tent that morning and gaze out at the giant peaks of the Himlung mountain range surrounded by a cloudless azure sky. I took a deep breath of the fresh, cold air and flopped back into my sleeping bag. What a way to wake up.

Kumar provided an unexpected breakfast of porridge followed by an omelette. The fuel that food provided me on these trips was crucial as I burned through so many calories each day. It meant I had to keep replenishing myself no matter what was on offer. After being at risk of turning into dal baht, things were definitely looking up in the menu department. Beetle was also already at home in our base camp – he'd been shadow practising his cricket shots before breakfast. The only worry was when he told me how geared up Ben was to do the climb. The previous evening, they had been talking in their shared tent and Ben had said he would drag himself up Himlung if he had to. I knew then that I had to tackle Ben's mindset over the coming days.

After finishing up, I headed back to my tent to sort out my washing when I noticed a man on a white horse heading over the horizon and up the valley towards us. As he got closer, there was no mistaking the telltale orange robes of a Buddhist monk.

'Arron, he's here!' I called out.

I turned around to our tent, but Arron was already emerging, wide-eyed. We both stood and watched the monk's slow progress, the only other sign of human life for miles.

'It's exactly how I imagined it would be,' Arron sighed.

I let him off as the lone monk on horseback, with mountains framing his approach, was a pretty stunning scene.

As the monk drew nearer, I could see a big grin below his old cotton Yankees baseball cap.

'*Namaste!*' Arron shouted, completely unaware that he sounded like an excited schoolgirl at a Harry Styles concert.

The seventy-year-old monk had arrived to deliver our *Puja*, the blessing that precedes the climb. It offers homage to the mountain and requests safe passage. I had seen this in mountaineering documentaries before and I was pretty excited to experience one firsthand. Not as excited as Arron, however.

Everyone at our base camp gathered as food and alcohol were offered at the foot of a *chorten*, which is a stone statue of symbolic importance in the Buddhist religion. *Chortens* are smaller than the *stupas* we saw in Phu village and are built with only stones and not mortar. Bigraj told us there couldn't be any statues of Buddha or the gods placed on them and, instead, images were carved directly into the stone. The *chorten* at Himlung Himal's base camp had been there for years and would have been built by a previous expedition. I found it comforting to think of the long line of porters, guides and mountaineers who had once stood in front of it.

The monk sat crossed-legged, facing the stone structure, and unrolled a fabric case containing a piece of worn parchment that he laid out in front of him. We all gathered around as the monk started chanting and Bigraj and Kaji made a fire from some green branches and herbs they had collected on their last day of trekking. We followed our Nepali brothers' lead, took fists full of rice, and sat down. An equal amount of spirituality and comical carnage ensued.

Dil and some of the porters started throwing rice at each other. Unsure if we were allowed to join in and not wanting to offend anyone, we waited while one of the porters started drinking one of the offering cans of Tuborg beer. Everyone was chattering away while the monk was happily working through his chants and ringing his bell at the appropriate parts in the text. I was struck by how different this was from the church services I used to attend as a kid, where you would be told off for even fidgeting. It was much more of a celebration. There was something quite magical and Nepalese about the whole event, which ended with the monk doing a shot of rum before passing it around.

We were all well and truly blessed.

CHAPTER 7

The Land of the Giants

We had ended the previous day before dinner and a few games of cards with some rope work and technical training on the snow slope behind the camp. It was important for everyone who wasn't used to basic mountaineering techniques to feel more comfortable with them. For Ben and Beetle, it was the first time they had got to put their crampons on.

I was lucky to have been introduced to technical climbing by the world-renowned mountaineer Leo Houlding. The introduction happened in 2021 when Berghaus put me in touch with him after I mentioned wanting to climb Mont Blanc. Being infinitely wise, Leo responded to the invitation by requesting that we first climb in the Lake District together. I later found out this was to check I wasn't a complete dick rather than to assess my skills. He had a family to raise and didn't want to spend his precious days stuck up a mountain with someone he was responsible for and couldn't escape from. He later told me he was relieved when I got out of my car at Scafell Pike in the Lakes and he clocked I had my baseball cap on backwards. Apart from Leo, I was pretty much the only person our age who still did that, so he apparently knew we would get along just fine. Or maybe, come to think of it, this meant we were both complete dicks . . . either way, we were going to get on.

Joining us on that climb was an excellent guide called Adrian Nelhams, who later also travelled over to Mont Blanc with us. When the three of us arrived in France, we soon realized the weather was far from ideal, so we quickly packed up and travelled to Switzerland, where we climbed two 4,000-metre mountains in a week. The Weissmies and the Allalinhorn were good introductions to the world of technical climbing and I was eager to learn about everything that came my way. Ascenders, figure-of-eight knots, daisy chains, carabiners, jumaring – I couldn't get enough of it. Everything Leo and Ade taught me I soaked up with an enthusiasm I hadn't experienced since my rugby days.

Before we abandoned Mont Blanc for the two Swiss mountains, Ade had taken me to Chamonix cemetery, known as the mountaineers' cemetery. He wanted to pay his respects before we began our climbs. As I peered at the gravestones, I quickly realized it was the resting place for mountaineering royalty. Some had reached old age and had enjoyed a lifetime of adventure, while others had sadly met an untimely death on the mountains.

The first person who ever climbed the Matterhorn, Edward Whymper, was buried in the cemetery, along with his two guides, a father and son team both named Peter Taugwalder. These three men reached old age, but their summit expedition in 1865 is another example of the dangers of the descent. On the way down, the most inexperienced climber, Charles Hudson, slipped and fell, taking three other climbers on the expedition with him. At age twenty-five and in the space of a day, Whymper summited the Matterhorn, which had perplexed mountaineering expeditions for years, lost four of his teammates and found himself as one of only three survivors. The mountains give and they take away in quick succession.

I remembered reading his book, *Scrambles Amongst the Alps,* covering that ascent, which haunted him for the rest of his life. In it, he said: 'Climb if you will, but remember that courage and strength are naught without prudence, and that a momentary negligence may destroy the happiness of a lifetime. Do nothing in haste; look well to each step; and from the beginning think what may be the end.' Whymper's words stayed with me and I always tried to remember them when I was in the mountains. They had guided him well and he had lived until he was seventy-one, after a lifetime of climbing mountain ranges as far-flung as the Canadian Rockies and Ecuador.

Our second day in the base camp was where the real work began, as it was time to start our acclimatization hikes. From what I've read, there have been accounts of 'mountain sickness' going back two thousand years, but it was in the nineteenth century, with the advent of hot air balloons, that medicine's understanding of acclimatization quickly advanced. Those first intrepid aeronauts discovered firsthand the effect on the human body of quickly moving upwards away from sea level. In 1862, a scientist named James Glaisher and an aeronaut, Henry Coxwell, flew in a hot air balloon to 8,800 metres above London – around the same height as Mount Everest. They could have even made it higher, but Glaisher passed out from the effects of altitude and that was his last barometer reading.

Acclimatization in the mountains involved a zigzag week of going up and down the slopes, which gave the body a chance to get used to the lower amounts of oxygen. There is a myth that physical fitness is a factor in the likelihood of acclimatization. This isn't true and it actually has more to do with genetics and the amount of time taken to acclimatize. How the person reacted to acclimatizing on previous occasions will also indicate how they should perform the next time, while factors like hydration and physical exertion also come into play. That was why Beetle and Ben were still somewhat untested. They were both extraordinarily fit but had not yet crossed over the 5,000-metre mark.

The plan for our first round of acclimatization was to head up to camp 1 at 5,400 metres and back again. Most larger mountains had a base camp and then camps 1–3, or even a camp 4 for the highest peaks, trailing up the route you climbed. They provided somewhere to rest for a few hours or overnight at different stages of the climb and to aid acclimatization. These numbered camps would have tents set up and usually somewhere to cook, but they wouldn't normally have the luxuries of a base camp with a communal area.

After some porridge and a quick kit check, we followed our two climbing guides, Kaji and Shyam, out of base camp, waving goodbye to the other climbing party from Kenya who had erected their tents near ours the previous evening. Our base camp was stationed at 4,900 metres and it was anticipated that climbing 600 vertical metres and back should take us around nine hours, depending on the conditions. It was a much-needed chance to get our legs used to a few more miles while also letting our bodies adapt to the increasingly thin air.

Himlung was first summited in 1992 by a Japanese team when it was first opened to climbers. Kaji and Shyam would be leading us up the safer north-west route, discovered in 2013, and this started around half a kilometre from base camp. Pleased to be on our way, we quickly crossed the scrubland that gently curved up into a lip, hiding the glacier we would have to cross behind it.

When we finally crested the ridge's edge, we all stopped and stared at what lay before us. I thought of the glacier I had crossed the previous year in Iceland with the Millimetres 2 Mountains beneficiaries. It had been precisely what you would expect from a glacier – a sparkling sheet of ice with a few sapphire-blue crevasses to gaze into. What we were facing that day was its much uglier big brother.

A hundred and fifty feet below us lay a dumping ground for boulders, rocks and scree that the mountain and valley had pushed from its slopes. There was no glittering ice, only a boulder field filled with pyramids of deposited rock, some twenty to thirty metres high, with no clear route through. A winter wonderland this was not; it was closer to a desiccated, abandoned mine.

On the far side, I picked out the Nepali porters who had set off before us. As the crow flew, it didn't seem too far from one side to the other, but as we descended on a sheer slope of loose stones, I quickly realized it would be no ordinary glacier crossing. I have crossed a fair few boulder fields since I started climbing mountains – they come with the territory of steep rock slopes mixed with gravity – but those piles of rubble were like nothing I had seen before. Not only would they pose a physical challenge, but they would create a mental one too. All it would take was one misplaced walking pole and we would be on a helicopter out of there.

As we carefully picked our way down the slope of the valley, I stopped to glance over at Ben. His gaze was fixed on his feet, concentrating hard to ensure he didn't have an early tumble. One of the more challenging elements both Ben and I faced was the lack of sensation in our legs, which affected our proprioception. This highly underrated sense is taken for granted by most people as it's often automatic and involves our body's ability to sense where each part of it is in relation to our surroundings. If you've ever stopped yourself from falling down the stairs, safely walked in the dark or nimbly weaved through a crowd without bumping into anyone, then you have the proprioception in all your muscles to thank. Because Ben and I can't feel where our legs are, it means we cannot always rely on proprioception to keep track of them. Instead, we might need visual confirmation of where we are guiding our legs or to have four points of contact with the earth through our legs and walking poles. This is particularly tricky in a boulder field where any of those points can wobble and even dislodge. On top of this, I also struggled with my balance because of the weakness in my hips and core. Long story short, boulder fields were absolute bastards for us.

Trying to keep my anxiety to myself, I dropped in behind Beetle and managed to make it to the bottom of the scree slope without a fall and stepped onto the glacier. Everything in the mountains plays with physics and your perception of your surroundings. Down on the glacier, we were Borrowers in the land of the giants. I picked my way forward, taking it slowly as there couldn't be any bravado when it came to those types of obstacles. With nearly every step something shifted or slipped underfoot. Most of the boulder fields I had crossed in the Alps got a fair bit of foot traffic, so the looser rocks had settled or been moved. At the base of Himlung, I quickly realized we were facing an enormous *and* unstable boulder field, as we were the first team to cross it in two years. The mental strain was huge as every movement had to be considered, planned and executed.

The only sounds for the next few hours were the sharp cracks of rockfall that had us all wincing in response and the occasional shouts when one of us began to slide on the scree. I spent nearly the entire time staring at my feet as I checked and rechecked their placement in a valley completely devoid of all plant and animal life. There weren't any buds of green life poking through the ground around my feet or walking poles, even though it was spring, and no moss or lichen lined the boulders. The only other living things were the eagles lazily circling above us; their constant presence made me wonder if they were waiting for one of us to drop.

After two hours of concentration levels akin to appearing on *University Challenge*, we made it to the towering slope of loose rocks on the other side. It was so steep we would need climbing ropes to help us scale it. The guides had anchored belay ropes the day before, so we put on our harnesses and hooked up before waiting to take turns jumaring up the slope. This meant the rope would support our weight and rather than hanging straight down, our feet would be at forty-five degrees on the slope. We would then use the jumar, a small hand-held device attached to the rope, to help pull our body weight up while our feet steadied us. Jumars are metal contraptions that look a bit like a saw handle with metal teeth running inside them and over the rope. This means you can only push them in one direction, in our case, upwards, and as long as you held onto them, you wouldn't slide down. Most importantly, while walking up a steep gradient, they meant you could use the rope to help pull you up for each step rather than relying solely on hiking poles or ice axes.

Kaji went first and expertly made his way up the slope, loose rocks cascading down at every step. We were all wearing helmets, but the rocks flying down were still large enough to do considerable damage, so we had to stand far from the firing line. Ben went next, then Beetle, and they both made it look relatively easy.

By the time it was my turn, the other expedition had come up behind us. The slope we were waiting to climb had created a bottleneck, a bit like the Hillary Step on Everest, where climbers had to queue to clip onto the single rope that would take them both up to and down from the summit. We had been chatting with the other team at base camp over the last day, but I was conscious that what they were about to witness might surprise them, as the way I did things in the mountains wasn't pretty. Feeling the pressure with another party standing around watching me, I hooked in and hauled myself up the first couple of metres, dragging my left leg with me. I've had to work out different ways to get through, over and around things, which often just relies on sheer determination. I'd be lying if I said it didn't bother me sometimes, but there was usually no room for self-consciousness in what was often a risky situation.

After a couple of metres of pulling myself up, I reached a boulder too big for me to step over. Hanging there indefinitely wasn't an option, so I tried to move around it by stretching my right leg to the side, hoping to shuffle my left leg over to meet it. It was at that moment my right foot gave way. Supported only by the rope, I swung hard to the side and my shoulder crunched into the scree, sending a shower of dust and pebbles downwards. I winced when I heard a couple of gasps from below.

'I'm fine,' I said quickly to try and alleviate any worry.

My ego had risen and I had been trying to move too fast. I took a couple of breaths, gathered myself, grabbed the knee loop sewn onto my trousers and carried on up the slope but at a slower pace and as safely as possible. It wasn't long until Ben's grinning face met me as he peered over the side. After a few more steps, I hauled myself over the lip and onto flat land.

'Clear!' I shouted to everyone below, so they knew the next person was safe to come up.

A few minutes later, Arron's head popped over the lip of the slope. We had made it through the glacier and now, with the team assembled, it was three hours to camp 1.

Although steep, the low grass and compact stones we were trekking across were a welcome respite from the boulder field and I felt myself starting to speed up. This time, it wasn't my ego raising its head. When I swung my leg without it getting caught on rocks or stones, I could walk at a decent pace, so much so that when I stopped a couple of hours later to gulp in some air, I realized the rest of the team was spread out behind me. It was a rare but incredible feeling to know I could still set the pace for the 'able bodies' from time to time. I knew those moments were short-lived, so I was determined to enjoy them while I could.

As I caught my breath and waited for the others, I noticed a herd of blue sheep grazing about forty metres away. All twelve of them were intent on not leaving the patch of grass they had discovered, so they monitored me rather than abandoning their lunch and skittering away. Besides, these high altitude operators were the favourite prey of snow leopards, so they had bigger things to worry about than a few wobbly *Homo sapiens*. It was strange to see wild animals so comfortable in the presence of humans, but it was a testament to how few they saw in the furthest reaches of the Himalayas.

The sun was high up in the sky, so I shielded my eyes to watch the boys' progress. As they approached, I realized Ben was breathing hard. When he reached me, he tripped and almost fell.

'Are you alright, mate?' I said, trying to help steady him.

'Yeah, fine, just struggling to catch my breath.'

I knew how he felt. The going was tough up there with the thin oxygen making every step feel like twenty.

'Do you want to rest for a bit or keep going?' I asked.

'Keep going.'

He was leaning heavily on his walking poles as he said it. I had anticipated his answer and knew it would have been mine, too. I took ten more steps, sat down, and took my bag off to get out some food. It was the only way I could think of to make Ben rest. After a short break where Ben was very quiet, we continued upwards.

Five hours after setting off from base camp, we decided to turn back. We were only a hundred vertical metres from camp 1, which was frustrating, but we wanted to ensure we got back before dark. The sun was still high in the sky, but it could trick people into believing there was plenty of daylight left if they wanted to go just a little further. Its rays were also beating down on us and the dry air meant we were all drinking more than we had anticipated. We were running low on water and I could tell I was starting to dehydrate. The biggest indication for me was when brain fog set in and my thoughts were slow and jumbled. It took me about half an hour to conclude that despite having drunk two litres, it just wasn't enough and heading back to base camp was the safest decision. My mind then latched on to the glacier we would have to cross again – this time, tired and dehydrated. There was no point in complaining, I just had to put my head down and get on with it.

Two hours later, we reached the almost vertical shale slope we had previously jumared up, which would lead us into the glacier. The Kenyan team was ahead of us, abseiling one by one back down to the land of the giants. Stuck at the back of the bottleneck, we would have to wait our turn.

'Rock!' someone from the other team shouted and everyone below them quickly moved out of the way.

The same warning shout happened repeatedly and our team looked at each other nervously. The sun had clearly melted the ice holding the scree surface together. This meant every step taken on it was dislodging something and the longer we waited, the more unstable it would get. We tried not to show our anxiety, but we were all nervous about what being held up for another half an hour would produce.

Finally, the other team was safely down and disappeared across the glacier. It was our turn. Beetle was called forward to clip in. As he stepped back onto a large boulder to position himself to start the descent, it suddenly shifted. With a scraping noise, his foot slid down and he cried out. His leg had dropped below the boulder and the only thing stopping it from crashing to the ground was his shin.

'Don't move!' I shouted to Beetle.

I'd spotted one of the other team below who had returned to

retrieve something they had dropped. They were 150 feet below the firing line. It was Beetle's shin or potentially someone's life.

Kaji and Shyam ran over and leant down on either side of Beetle to try and take some of the weight.

'Rock!' we all screamed to the man below.

He was clearly exhausted, hadn't been concentrating and had wandered underneath Beetle. You should never walk underneath a person abseiling because of the loose rock they might dislodge. A look of alarm crossed the man's face and he hastily scrabbled out of the way. His progress was painfully slow as his feet skidded beneath him.

'Are you okay?' I shouted to Beetle, who was straining not to let the boulder fall.

He was sweating from the effort and the pain in his leg and could only give a small nod. All his concentration was focused on keeping that one boulder from falling.

Time stood still as the boulder lurched a couple of centimetres forward and Beetle groaned, his leg shaking with the strain.

It had only been seconds but felt like hours when 'Clear!' finally came from below.

'One, two, three,' Kaji said.

Beetle moved his leg and the guides let go of the boulder simultaneously.

Everyone watched silently as the huge rock crashed to the ground below, chunks splintering off in multiple directions. It had been too close for comfort for all of us.

Fortunately, Beetle's hardy Scottish shin had no lasting damage and he continued his descent. I was last down, but there was no time to rest. The echoing sound of rocks crashing down the sides of the valley was impossible to ignore. It sent a clear message that we really weren't safe. The best place to avoid the shrapnel was in the middle of the glacier, but we had to cross half of the boulder field to get there and didn't have the same fresh minds to navigate it. Heads down, we started our ascent of the first pile of rubble.

Halfway up, I missed my footing after misjudging my step from the lack of sensation from my leg. I managed to twist before I hit the ground, fortunately landing on my shoulder rather than my face. Learning to fall had become a necessity, first through rugby, then again after my accident. If there were awards for falling over, I'd be well-decorated by this point in my life. I checked myself over and there were just a few bloody knuckles and a small cut on my elbow. Considering my surroundings, it seemed like a good outcome, but judging by the looks on Kaji and Shyam's faces, they disagreed.

'It's nothing, really,' I said. 'Don't worry about it, this sort of thing always happens.'

My words gave them little comfort. For the rest of the boulder field, Shyam stuck by my side, testing every boulder for me and guiding me on where to place my feet. His help was needed in the final hour back to base camp, as concentrating was becoming increasingly difficult. We had all fallen silent and the combination of fatigue and dehydration was taking its toll. My head was pounding and my vision had become blurred. I was well and truly in The Bin – with the lid shut on me and perhaps someone kicking it over – and I knew that another mistake could end the trip.

We reached base camp in silence ten hours after leaving. Slumping to the floor in the communal tent, I began to shiver. My body had gone into shock. A blanket was wrapped around my shoulders and Kumar handed me a cup of masala tea, which Rabin topped up with extra sugar. I didn't protest; I couldn't even thank them as I hadn't been able to speak for the past hour. I sipped the sweet liquid while trying to get my head around what had happened. It had been one of the most mentally demanding days I'd had in the mountains. For once, I was glad I was out of contact with Lois and my mum because if they had heard about what had happened, they would have been incredibly worried. The state I was in wasn't necessarily because of the physical exertion, it was primarily the mental challenge of concentrating so hard for ten hours. I was neurologically exhausted.

'I don't understand what has happened,' Kaji said as he topped up my tea. 'I have summited Himlung five times and I have never seen this part so dangerous.'

All of us were shaken by the day's events, especially Bigraj and his team. Himlung had been appealing as it was so far from the main routes, but no one had been there for two years because of the impact of Covid-19 shutting down Nepalese tourism. I took little comfort in knowing it wasn't our lack of skill or fitness that had impacted the day. Instead, it was a massive wake-up call for everyone about the scale of the challenge that lay ahead. The glacier that stood between us and the other camps was a gnarly, dangerous place and it would impact our entire acclimatization process if we had to cross it every time we needed to get to camp 1 or 2.

It was our first day on Himlung and the mountain had kicked our ass. We would have to go back to the drawing board.

CHAPTER 8

Getting Out of The Bin

I blinked open my eyes, then quickly closed them again. My head was pounding and the sunlight seeping into my tent made me wince. Opening one eye again to peer at my phone, I tentatively checked my vitals on my Garmin and Aura apps. Scanning the information logged on my heart rate variability and body temperature, I was relieved not to have woken up in a worse state following the trauma of the previous day. Nine hours of sleep had definitely helped.

It was a recovery day and given that it was only 6 a.m., I really didn't want to get up. But I also knew the reason I had a headache was due to dehydration and I had to get some fluids on board. Shaking the bottle beside my bed roll revealed that the little water I had left was frozen solid.

After slowly peeling myself out of my sleeping bag, I grabbed my down jacket, strapped on my orthotic and hobbled over to the kitchen tent in search of fluids. All of our water was collected from the snow melt stream that ran through the camp. It had to be boiled first to purify it, so as I pushed open the kitchen tent door, I prayed our cook was already up. With great relief, I was met with the moist heat produced by pots of water on the boil. Steam rose to the top of the tent and small droplets occasionally lost their battle with gravity and dripped back into the pots underneath. Kumar ushered me in and put a chair close to one of the gas burners that had a bubbling saucepan above it. It wasn't quite the same as sitting around a campfire, but I appreciated the thought. Fold-up chairs lined the tent as this was where the porters came to relax with Kumar, their good friend and the keeper of our food.

Communicating through grins and pointing, Kumar handed me a glass of water before showing me around his rustic yet impressive setup, of which he was rightfully proud. Our supplies for the next week were neatly stacked in what looked to be a very precise order. In a box in the corner of the kitchen, I noticed a flash of angled silver that was not the round curves of the other pots and pans. My heart leapt and, with Kumar's permission, I pulled out my prize – an Italian moka pot that could brew coffee on a stove. My friend Eddy, who ran Round Hill Roastery, had kindly supplied us with some decent coffee, which I believed was an essential part of any expedition. Or any day. We just hadn't found a suitable brewing method to do it justice, but that had now changed.

Kumar and I sat together as we sipped our first cups of coffee. There is a common language in sharing a hot drink and this traversed any verbal barriers we might have had. I took my second cup outside and headed out of camp to find somewhere to sit and take it all in. The sun had risen above Himlung and, with the warmth on my face, I thought about our situation. The glacier had caught me by surprise the previous day as it was much harder than we had anticipated. We would have to cross it at least twice again, possibly more depending on our acclimatization hikes, and it was only the first part of our journey. I would still need the energy to concentrate for another few days and I couldn't see how that was possible. It was also a completely different beast from what we had anticipated, and even the guides were surprised at how much Himlung had changed in the two years it hadn't been climbed. All of my research into Himlung stated it wasn't a technical climb and was one of the more accessible 7,000-metre peaks. There were clearly technical sections to it, which I was fine with, but the fact it hadn't been climbed for two years meant the surface was much less stable and we didn't know what to expect further up. I took my coffee cup back to the kitchen tent and, on the way, passed Ben, who was also deep in thought.

After our gruelling previous day, Kumar had arranged a treat for us. I went over to the shower tent, got undressed, pulled the bucket handle above me and out came hot water. My first hot – or even warm – shower since leaving Kathmandu. That was what all the bubbling saucepans were for; Kumar had got up early so he could gift each of us a hot shower. I took my time as I knew it would probably be the first and last pleasant shower until we got back to Kathmandu.

That evening, the sky was completely clear and there was a blanket of stars – pinpricks of light so close together they could barely be picked out. I sat outside my tent and stared up at the midnight blue sky that turned to a shade of forest green when you looked at it through a camera lens. Sitting there, I witnessed what we would have looked up at hundreds of years ago before light pollution masked the sky from us. Every few seconds, a shooting star sparked across the sky, reminding me they were not as rare as we think; we just had to travel a bit further to see them. In cities and towns, these astronomical light shows were still happening above, they were just hidden from us.

After a while, Beetle came to sit with me.

'I still can't get used to it,' he said.

'What? The cold?'

'No, the internal monologue in my head disappearing. It's just gone. I'm so used to my brain constantly churning out ideas and thoughts and they're not there anymore. I've never experienced this and it's a bit scary.'

I grinned at him. 'Don't worry, it'll come back again. The voice will kick back in when all the emails, calls and busyness start up. Just try and enjoy this whilst you can.'

A few minutes later, I added, 'I've always noticed when that layer of surface chatter is cleared, it allows you to think more deeply and reach levels of thought you haven't accessed before. I use this time to consider what is important to me, where I am going and how I can realign myself with my purpose. It's not that your mind switches off; it switches quantity of thought for quality of thought.'

'Have you decided to change something then?' Beetle asked.

I smiled. It was a good question. 'I might need to, but I haven't quite worked out what it is.'

As I stared at the night sky, the contrast of the physical output these climbs demanded compared with the mental clarity and calmness gained amazed me. In those moments, I was truly present in my surroundings and life. Every year, people asked me if I would have some downtime by going to a beach or sitting by a swimming pool. But that wasn't what rejuvenated me; being in the mountains gave me the headspace to realign with my purpose and feel ready for our busy world again.

*

The following morning, after our welcome day of rest, the team gathered in the main tent to discuss our approach. After some deliberation with the guides, we decided to tweak our summit plan due to the danger of the glacier crossing. We would now spend an extra day at base camp before heading to camp 1 and acclimatizing there before the summit push, to minimize the necessary glacier crossings. I was naturally relieved as the glacier was most likely the place where either Ben or I would have a fall. There was a price to it, though, which was that we'd be shortening the acclimatization phase before the summit attempt, as we wouldn't be returning to base camp, which was now scheduled for 31st March rather than 2nd April. It wasn't ideal, but we had all coped well with the altitude so far and all we could do was hope it would continue.

As we had changed our summit day, I knew I had a legitimate reason to break our plan not to contact the outside world. We needed to update everyone back in the UK and it justified the eye-watering expense of around £15 for one message. I quickly updated Lois on our altered plans, copied over the message I had previously meant to send her from Meta and sincerely apologized for it not having reached her earlier. I signed off saying I would call once we were safely back at base camp.

Feeling much better after sending a message to Lois and more rested after our day off, I suggested to the boys that we got kitted up and went on a training hike behind base camp. Before we left, I wandered over to Ben, who was sitting outside of his tent.

'I'm sorry you won't be joining us today, mate,' I said, as he stared glumly across the base camp. 'Arron told me about your foot.'

When we returned from crossing the boulder field, Aaron noticed Ben had been hobbling and was reluctant to put weight on his right foot. Arron had asked him about it, but Ben had brushed it off. Concerned, Aaron had demanded to see Ben's foot as he knew how stubborn young men can be when ignoring pain. Once his boot and sock had been peeled off, it was clear the ulcer Ben had been managing back in the UK had become considerably worse. After looking at it, Ben realized he would have to spend several days resting. It had also prompted us all to agree to show at least one other person our feet at the end of the day to ensure no one was soldiering on when they should have been resting up.

'It's probably best I stay off it,' Ben said, 'but I wish I was joining you.'

'What are you going to do for the day?' I asked.

'Rest up and listen to podcasts. There's not much else I can do, really, is there?'

I fully understood his frustration. One of the most annoying things about our types of injury is that they occasionally demand periods of rest, which can be frustrating for people whose natural temperaments enjoy being active. It was doubly frustrating if you had been dreaming of summiting a mountain and couldn't even get your walking boot on.

After promising to spend the evening with him, Bigraj, Arron, Beetle and I grabbed our boots and crampons and headed to the foot of the snow slope – the opposite direction to the dreaded glacier. So far, our time at base camp hadn't involved much snow and we therefore needed time to practise the often-unappreciated art of wading through snow.

As soon as we set off, we knew it would be tough. The snow

was very soft on the lower slopes and it wasn't long before we were knee deep. At just five foot five, half of Bigraj disappeared. Deep snow conditions are the ones I've traditionally always dreaded because I can't lift my foot vertically. When trekking through snow this deep, most people will lift their legs high and stomp through it. This wasn't an option for me, so I lifted my leg a little lower and pushed it forward like a human snowplough. But, despite my fears, I made progress. It wasn't pretty and there were plenty of feral noises coming out of me but, thanks to the loop adaptation on my trousers, which meant I could haul my leg upwards, and the filed-down crampon on my left foot, which meant my foot wasn't getting caught in the snow and ice, I made a decent go of it.

Half-grimacing, half-smiling, I turned to Bigraj, who was staring at me.

'I don't believe it!' he said. 'You can move so much easier than on Mera.'

'I know!' I responded, pleased with my progress.

It had been two-and-a-half years since we had climbed Mera Peak together and, judging by Bigraj's reaction, there had definitely been some improvement.

Three hours later, we decided to turn back. The heat of the day was penetrating the snow and we were sinking further down, which meant we were all exerting vast amounts of energy to take even a couple of steps. There was a balance to strike between training and energy conservation because, in just two days, we would be crossing the glacier again and beginning our ascent of Himlung.

As we descended the snow slope with the sun in our eyes and smiles on our faces, I walked next to Arron.

'How was Ben's toe looking when you checked it this morning?' I asked.

'I haven't seen it yet, but last night it still wasn't right,' he responded. 'His doctor told him before he left for Nepal that if it got bad, there was a possibility he could lose his toe.'

Ben was a seriously tough boy and I knew how much he wanted to climb Himlung, but I hoped he also appreciated having ten toes. He had stayed on top of the ulcer for the past week, but that morning, I could tell he was worried about it. I hoped Ben would continue to make rational decisions regarding his foot. The last thing I wanted was for him to do something he regretted.

'It's not just his toe I'm worried about,' Arron said. 'It's where his head is at as well.'

It was a relief to hear I wasn't the only one concerned by how much Ben had riding on this trip.

'If he's out for the count,' Arron continued, 'I genuinely think he will be devastated.'

'It's been worrying me too. The last thing we wanted was to put him in a worse place mentally than before he left. What really concerns me is if he does join us for the summit push, he will ignore what his instincts are telling him and keep on to the top whatever happens.'

'Yeah, we'll just have to keep an eye on him.'

'It's good you've started inspecting everyone's feet, by the way.'

Arron grinned. 'That reminds me, I need to see yours when we get back. I didn't have the time to check them this morning.'

'It's so weird we've started staring at each other's feet every day. I don't know how I'm going to explain this to Lois.'

'Best not to, mate. Once Lois and Antonia find out, they'll never let us live it down.'

'Yeah, probably should keep that to ourselves.'

An hour later, we reached base camp and headed straight to Ben's tent. He wasn't there and we eventually found him in the communal tent, sitting with Kaji and Shyam.

'It's looking good, boys!' he shouted to us through a big-bearded grin. 'I thought I was stuffed, but there's a good chance now.'

'Show us then,' I said, wanting to check he wasn't being overly optimistic.

We all crowded around and Ben's toe was indeed looking much better.

'One more day off my feet and we're on!' he beamed.

It was hard not to get swept up in his enthusiasm. To celebrate, we all got into our summit suits and huddled in the communal tent around my iPad mini to watch the latest *Drive to Survive* series, which I'd downloaded before leaving Kathmandu.

It was clear I had finally acclimatized to the base camp height of 4,900 metres when I had my first decent night's sleep. When I woke up the following day, I felt like a different person and my brain was finally functioning at a relatively normal pace – just in time to head higher and scramble it again.

Our trekking guide, Dil, had been particularly interested in my coffee-brewing method and would now start his day by grinding the fresh beans I had brought with me. The Nepalese are not known for their love of coffee as they usually only have the freeze-dried variety, but Dil had taken a shine to both the ceremony of grinding the beans and the rich brews it produced. I didn't mind handing over my morning ritual, as it meant a bubbling pot would be waiting for me when I entered the kitchen tent.

After a strong cup, it was time to get our kit organized for the start of our final climb up Himlung the following day. All our tents and kit bags were emptied, the contents spread out and the meticulous packing process began again.

The challenge we were facing was to take everything we might need and only that. We didn't want to increase the weight we would carry by even a gram, but this had to be finely balanced with not wanting to be caught short. We were entering the next stage of our climbing experience, where the porters were carrying our tents but we were responsible for carrying everything else we would need, including our summit suits, sleeping bags, food, water and roll mats. Our light rucksacks were gone and we would each be laden with a bag that weighed between 10–12 kg. The porters would only carry our tents to camp 2 and the mountain guides had their own supplies to carry. We were, therefore, in the middle ground of not being laden with a tent but nowhere near as free as we had been for the past week and a half. To say it was daunting was an understatement. The glacier had been difficult enough with a small bag containing some food and water. The following day, I would have to cross it with a full rucksack.

Arron and I stood outside our tent and looked at our conundrum. We had limited bag space and a great deal to pack.

'Perhaps if we roll them rather than folding?' I said hopefully, looking at some clothing.

'Roll while leaning on them at the same time to try to decrease the air pockets?' Arron responded.

'Good idea. Shall we organize the food and supplements next?'

He nodded. Having enough energy and staying hydrated was critical in the environments we would face, not only because of the extreme cold but also because we wanted to avoid brain fog from dehydration or lack of calories, as it could endanger our lives. A reduced capacity to make decisions naturally led to poor decisions. We didn't want to be caught short, but the payoff was always going to be the weight. We were aiming for the sweet spot of minimum weight for maximum energy. It was only fair that I packed with Arron, as we both knew he would be carrying most of my fuel to increase my chances on summit day. It was safe to say I would be leaving the cheese board back at base camp.

The weight restrictions also impacted me in terms of medical equipment. As I couldn't take many spares of my Conveens and bags, I would have to rely on certain things not malfunctioning. It opened me up to trouble on the mountainside as it wasn't as if I could borrow any of those items from the others.

'What are we going to do with our summit boots?' Arron said. 'Do you think we could just wear them the entire time?'

The summit boots I'd always had mixed feelings about stared back at me. They were enormous and would take up so much precious space.

'We will have to carry them as I'll never get across the glacier in mine. The less time spent in heavier footwear, the better for me.'

My TurboMed also didn't attach to my summit boots, so when I started to wear them, I knew I wouldn't be able to lift my left foot unless I physically pulled it upwards.

Arron slung on his enormous pack with all our food supplies plus his kit and took a few turns around base camp with it.

Dil spotted him from the kitchen tent and shouted out, 'Eh, it's Donkey Number 19!'

Arron grinned at his new nickname. The eighteen donkeys that had carried all our equipment up to base camp were now safely back in Meta village, but luckily we had a new one with us.

When Arron returned to our tent, I picked up my own bag to check its weight. It wasn't as light as I had been hoping despite Donkey Number 19 carrying all my heavier items.

We checked our kit a second time and then a third before retiring to the communal tent for an afternoon of podcasts, reading and general downtime. Spirits were high among the team, but I couldn't stop thinking about the glacier we would cross again in the morning. The one that had nearly finished me off the first time.

CHAPTER 9

Low, Medium and High Consequences

At breakfast, everyone was unusually silent. Even Beetle, who could always be relied on to start a lively conversation, was uncharacteristically taciturn and Dil's wide smile didn't raise any others.

'Here we are then, lads,' I said, trying to elicit some sort of response. 'It's the big one today.'

There were a few nods, some half-finished sentences and then we all fell silent again.

It was like the changing room before a big rugby game. Adrenaline was clearly in the air, but the uncertainty over what would happen in the next few days had put everyone on edge. I had been there plenty of times and the answer was always the same: you don't know what will happen. All you can do is trust in your preparation and give it your best shot.

The day on the glacier had rattled us all but, even though I had struggled the most with it, I was more confident than the rest of the group about our second approach. Overnight, I had reasoned that we only had to cross it once more before we climbed the mountain – or not, depending on what unfolded. We'd also already successfully crossed the glacier in both directions. It was therefore familiar and we had a clearer route across it. The unknown can affect your mindset and build something up to be worse than it is, but we no longer had that to contend with.

Just before we were about to leave, I walked around the base camp as I knew it would be a while before I saw it again. The summit push would take at least three days, possibly up to five depending on the weather and how we were coping with the altitude. I might not have been worried about the glacier that morning, but I was concerned about the amount of kit I had packed to get me through that length of time. The heavier the bags were, the more exertion would be required, which could easily affect my chances of acclimatizing.

Ready to leave and with our bags full to the brim, we heaved them onto our backs. Arron and I stared at each other in silent agreement that it would be one hell of a day. Ben's toe was still on the mend so we had distributed his kit among the guides, but Arron, Beetle and I had packs that could form the foundations for a new stadium. It was by far the heaviest bag I'd put on since my accident and we would be climbing 600 vertical metres above 5,000 metres. Even if I did make it to camp 1 with that monstrosity strapped to my back, it would probably spell the end of my summit attempt. Something had to be done about it before we set off.

As Ben had commandeered the guides' spare rucksack space and Beetle had a bag full of heavy camera equipment, there was only one solution – Arron, aka Donkey Number 19. If anyone could deal with a bit of extra weight, it was a six foot three, 100 kg fitness fanatic with, most importantly, two working legs. Arron happily took my water and food from me, dropping my pack weight from around 15 kg to 12 kg. I was hopeful it would make a significant difference, but a part of me worried it would not.

Waving goodbye to our trekking guides and porters, we set off up the slope to the glacier's edge. From now on, it was just me, Ben, Beetle, Arron, Bigraj, Shyam and Kaji. None of the porters or trekking guides would be accompanying us all the way to the summit as they were not expected or qualified to climb the entire mountain. As we set off, I wished we had been able to afford extra climbing guides to carry our rucksacks as some mountaineers did, but that wasn't an option for this trip. We would just have to make the best of it.

It was our plan for one of our climbing guides, Shyam, to go ahead and help fix the lines with the Kenyan team, so it wasn't long until he became just a speck in the distance. When multiple teams are in a base camp, it has become standard practice in the last couple of decades for each team to supply a climbing guide to help fix the ropes up the mountain. These fixed ropes are the ones the rest of the team clips into to prevent them from falling. There wouldn't be fixed ropes all the way up Himlung, just in the stretches where there would be a serious drop to contend with if one of us fell. Cooperating like this meant the job didn't need to be done multiple times by multiple teams and would conserve the guides' energy.

When we reached the top of the rock-strewn glacier, it looked just as ugly as I had remembered. But this time, I could also pick out the route we had previously taken, removing some of the guesswork from the journey ahead. We made it safely down the scree slope and I was pleased to find that trekking up and down the mounds of rubble wasn't as treacherous as a few days before, as most of the loose boulders had found their place after two expedition teams had stomped on them multiple times.

Going up the first thirty-metre rubble mound, I found that when I leant to the left or right, the movement was compounded by my heavy pack, which also leant in that direction, pulling me further to the side than I had intended. As I started the descent, I took it slowly and all four contact points through my legs and walking poles were even more essential. One rubble mound down, I sighed, realizing we had another twenty to go.

As we slowly crossed the glacier, the silence from breakfast returned. Trying to lighten the mood, I searched the back catalogue of songs stored in my head for one with 'rock' or 'boulder' in it.

The opening lines of Status Quo's *Rockin' All Over the World* struggled out from my dry vocal cords.

Fortunately, Ben jumped straight on backing vocals and the boys spent the next half hour picking up where I had left off, while I focused on getting enough oxygen into my lungs to tackle the next rubble pile. All the time, I told myself to slow down and take it carefully, as there was no room for my ego to rise.

When I climbed in the mountains, I was rarely scared of a dramatic drop where time slowed down. The type of free fall where I would be left praying the rope snapped into place and the ice screw was secured deep enough to take my weight. Instead, what occupied my mind most of the time was the risk of a simple rolled ankle. It's easy to do on uneven ground and the consequences would be trip-ending. Sure, I would be fine after a week or two of putting my leg up on a coffee table and watching Netflix, but there were no second chances to summit on these trips. You'd paid for your summit window and if you missed it, you had to wait for the next season to try again – *if* you could afford to try again. That was why we were religiously checking each other's feet for pressure sores and frostbite, because it was the little things that would most likely upend our chance to summit. Our regular toe inspections were particularly important the higher we got, as the altitude makes feet swell. It meant our trekking boots had to be a size bigger to accommodate this and it was only recently that the boys no longer needed to wear double socks to keep theirs on.

During my trip to Switzerland with Leo and Adrian the previous year, I had learnt about low, medium and high consequences, which were terms climbers used when they don't want to mention the word 'death'. Low consequence was possibly some bruises or an embarrassing stumble you would later laugh about. Medium consequence meant if you fell in that particular section, it would likely result in a trip-ending injury, or it would hurt a lot, but you were unlikely to die. High consequence meant if you fell at that point, you would almost certainly die. It took me around two days to work out these meanings and it was reassuring that all the times Leo had said 'high consequence' on our trip, I hadn't made the immediate leap to 'I might die'. Instead, I just knew I didn't want to fall at that particular stretch. Some of these areas might not seem that risky to the untrained eye, but they can include things above you as well as below, such as avalanches or rockfalls. We were firmly in the 'medium consequence' zone in the glacier, but I was desperate not to end my trip there.

After a couple of hours, we finally jumared up the scree slope and I landed belly-down in my low-consequence comfort zone of relatively even ground. Before making our way up to camp 1, we all dug into our packs for a quick snack of a bag of nuts and half a salami. On a summit push, the snacks weren't particularly nutritious as they must have a high calorie and fat content when you were exerting so much energy. I had learnt the hard way that chocolate wasn't always the best option when I nearly broke a tooth on a Galaxy bar, as I hadn't realized how easily chocolate froze. The snacks also couldn't be easily perishable, so we would have to rely on supplements and freeze-dried food for the necessary nutrients in the following days.

We set off again and even though this was where I had shot off the previous day, I stayed with the rest of the gang as I wanted to keep an eye on Ben and Beetle and I knew my rucksack would make every step ten times as difficult. Arron had faced high altitude with a heavy pack back on Mera, but this was a new experience for the other two. The first indication they were finding it tough was when they stopped talking. It was incredible the difference the weight we were carrying made. One kilogram might not seem like much, but it makes a difference when you multiply that by ten-, fifteen- or twenty-thousand steps.

We were about four hours into our six-hour push when Beetle turned to me, his face shining with sweat and said, 'This is fucking ridiculous. I get it now. I found it relatively easy up until this point, but this . . . This is fucked!'

I smiled and just responded with, 'Welcome.'

High-altitude mountaineering *is* suffering. It strips you down to the point where every other word is an expletive, as it is the only way to explain what you are going through. Every step was a struggle and in the space of a few hours, we were accelerated into old age when every breath never quite gave us enough oxygen, so we would gasp for another. It is certainly not for everyone, but for me, it is the ultimate test of character and resilience and the rewards are unrivalled. You discover things about yourself you never knew existed and develop areas you have always wanted to strengthen.

Six hours after leaving base camp, we finally crested a ridge and saw the seven tents that made up camp 1. My focus had been directed towards my feet for so long that I hadn't really taken stock of where we were, but we briefly stopped to take it in. Camp 1 was perched on a ledge of loose rock and the terrain we had to cross to get to it was more volcanic and largely free of snow. The wind picked up and I tried to record a short video diary, but its blustering sound covered most of my words.

As we took our last steps into camp 1, the first thing we did was shrug off our packs and let them drop to the ground. We were then free to fully take in our surroundings. Yet again, we were stunned into silence. In every direction were mountain ranges and we were perched on a ledge hanging over the side of a giant peak. Way above us, the rocky mountainside gave way to a sapphire-blue icefall and below us, the valley we had climbed stretched away towards the Annapurna region. We really were up among the gods.

Outside one of the bright orange tents, Bigraj pulled a burner from his pack and started to melt some snow to make tea. As he did this, I noticed two figures making their way down from above. As they got closer, I saw a stagger in their step. When they were a few metres away, it became clear it was Shyam and one of the Kenyan team's climbing guides and that they were struggling. They slumped next to Bigraj and Kaji quickly poured them some tea. They started talking quickly in Nepali and I could tell by the amount of frowning that things weren't good. Bigraj soon translated for us and the news from up high was that the snow conditions were very soft, so much so that even the professional Nepalese climbers couldn't reach the summit. They had been waist-deep in snow, which was unheard of that early in the season.

I leant back, cradling my tea. It didn't look good for our expedition if even the professional climbers could not summit. Tiredness engulfed me. It all seemed so futile. Even though I knew not summiting was a potential outcome, I felt a bit dejected after spending a year planning the trip.

Ben came and sat next to me. 'We've still got a chance.'

'Perhaps,' I said. 'If there is a big freeze overnight, it might change the snow conditions.'

'I've got faith in us,' Ben said, staring out over the view.

I nodded. All we could do was wait until the morning.

With Kumar safely back at base camp, the next stretch of our journey would rely entirely on freeze-dried meals to keep us going. They might sound pretty grim, but a few of them were quite tasty and the following morning, I tucked into freeze-dried porridge, brought alive with some boiling water, and had freeze-dried chilli waiting for me in the evening.

After breakfast, we still had an hour before we had to leave, so I took myself off to the ledge overhanging the valley to watch the sunlight cresting the mountain range. The news of the snow conditions higher up had unsettled me and I needed to put it into perspective just like I had done with my accident. Being a professional sportsperson for so many years always instilled a sense of competitiveness and a need for accomplishment in me. It's pretty difficult to devote yourself entirely to a sport without those two things in place. However, I had always tried not to take that attitude to the mountains. Yes, it would be great if Ben and I were the first people with paraplegia and quadriplegia to climb above 7,000 metres, but that was never the intended point of the expedition. It wasn't a fail or succeed scenario. But a small part of me still intensely wanted this to be what we came away with and I would be lying if I said it never crossed my mind. I also knew it might occupy my oxygen-depleted mind if I didn't try to address it. So, I tackled it in the way I dealt with most things of that nature: the simple act of feeling grateful for what I did have rather than focusing on what I didn't.

After half an hour of sitting quietly by myself, I felt much better. I had let my mind drift and the stillness of the freezing cold morning soothed me. I was experiencing one of those moments where I was outside of myself and thinking, 'How the hell have you ended up here?' Never mind how I had ended up there having been told I would never walk again, but even if the accident hadn't happened, my life would have looked very different without the impetus it gave me to challenge myself in a different way. By now, I would have retired from the sport and would probably have been working in London, too busy commuting and putting in ten-hour shifts to think about mountains or mindfulness. Most days, I thanked that swimming pool for giving me the opportunity for a very different life. I was even partway through making a documentary about what had happened. Sometimes, the moment that changed the entire course of your life was the best thing that ever happened to you. I had learnt in recent years not to have too rigid a plan, not get hung up on expecting things or stressing about where I needed to be in two years, five years or, in this case, three days. Feeling better, I pushed myself to my feet and returned to our tents. It was time to move on.

That day, we planned to climb towards camp 2 on our final acclimatization hike. We were all tired from the previous afternoon, but despite the altitude gain, everyone had got some decent sleep, which at this height was around three to four hours each night. I knew once we got higher, the altitude would start interfering with my sleep even more. Waking up every twenty minutes gasping for breath is no fun. Also, with less oxygen in our blood, the body's ability to recover is significantly hampered. Effectively, the longer you spent in high-altitude environments, the weaker you got, so it was a balancing act between spending time high up to acclimatize but not so much time that your body became detrimentally weak. 'Climb high and sleep low' was usually the approach to try and achieve this. However, this meant that by the time you went for the summit, you had already climbed the mountain a few times.

The fourth and final round of acclimatization took us up a steep scree slope and we were certainly glad not to be carrying the heavy packs we had left at camp 1. However, my relief was short-lived when I remembered that the next day we would be doing the same climb again but with a 12 kg pack on.

Every fifteen minutes, I would stop to turn around and check on the others. Arron was directly behind me and managing to keep up despite the extra weight he was carrying with my food and water. Beetle was clearly enjoying the relative freedom of a lighter pack and had stopped a couple of times to fly the drone around to capture the panoramic shots of seven specks in a vast landscape of snow and ice. Behind him, Ben was in a position similar to me. He was struggling to raise his right leg but was trying to power up the slope. I recognized the determined set to his features but was concerned about the energy he was expending.

An hour later, we reached our final destination, which was a rocky ledge next to the glacier we would have to cross the following day. It was our first look at the icefall we would have to cross to reach camp 2 and the rest of the mountain. Ben and Beetle had never been this close to an icefall and the giant shards stretching above and below us were undoubtedly impressive. To our left was a pristine snow slope and when I peered over the edge, I immediately pulled back again, my heart racing at the shock of what lay below. Next to us, the gentle slope masked a gaping crevasse. The dark mass looked like a hungry mouth, ready to swallow anything that went near it.

At 5,800 metres, we would soon turn around and head back to camp 1, but I could see the fixed lines disappearing into the ice jungle, which was firmly a 'high consequence' zone. But one we had to pass, as on the other side lay our route up to the summit of Himlung Himal.

'It looks gnarly, eh?' I said to Arron, who was sitting next to me.

Arron glanced behind him. 'I'm not exactly excited about that bit. All I can hear is rocks falling and there are lots of ropes, which tends to mean something "special" is about to happen.'

I smiled. 'And by special, you mean *safe* special, not *dangerous* special.'

'Yup, definitely *safe* special. That's what I meant.'

Three hours later, we arrived back in camp 1 without any major hiccups. We were all tired and hungry and I immediately set upon the freeze-dried chilli I had been looking forward to. My belly full of freeze-dried food and hot water, I sat and watched the sunset with Ben. It wasn't quite the romantic occasion it might sound like because, after ten minutes, I demanded to see his toe before the sunlight disappeared. Pleased that the ulcer was still dry, we both sat in silence for a bit.

'Okay, I have a question for you,' I said.

'Go on,' Ben responded, his interest piqued.

'What's your best mistake?'

He looked at me sheepishly and grinned. 'That's an easy one. Evie getting pregnant.'

'What? When did Evie get pregnant?'

I was floored. Normally I use this question as a way for people to reframe what is going on in their lives, but it seemed like there was something much bigger going on.

'She told me at the airport, right before we got on the plane to Nepal.'

'Bloody hell! And you've kept this to yourself the entire time? I don't know how you did it.'

'I haven't told anyone else except you. I haven't even been able to message anyone back home.'

'Congratulations, mate. I'm so pleased for you.'

He gave a wide smile. 'Evie had only just found out and she wasn't going to tell me until I got back as she didn't want it to stop me going, but then she couldn't hold it in. I'm glad she did tell me.'

'Well, that's certainly the best mistake I've ever heard. I'm really happy for you, mate.'

We sat quietly and I thought about all that Ben had been through the last couple of weeks and what he had kept to himself.

It was Ben who eventually broke the silence. 'Ed, I'm going to be a dad.'

CHAPTER 10

Overt and Hidden Dangers

The next day, we woke up to the beginning of our third week in Nepal. In that time, we had travelled hundreds of kilometres and scaled over 3,000 vertical metres into one of the most isolated parts of the world. Not bad for fourteen days of work.

Bigraj had suggested an early start to our climbing guides, as he thought it would be best to maximize our time at camp 2 to try and increase our chances of getting some sleep there. Kaji and Shyam had vetoed this. They preferred for us to have the opportunity of a lie-in at camp 1, as they reasoned there was more chance of us sleeping if we were at a lower altitude. It was their call. Even though Bigraj owned the company hiring them, once we got into the mountains they ran the show when it came to our route and timetable. It was their job to try and keep everyone as safe as possible. We didn't complain about the chance for a lie-in, but Ben and I had been waking up with the sunrise anyway, so the extra hour or two in a sleeping bag was wasted on us. On the other hand, Beetle and Arron probably wouldn't have woken up even if there was an avalanche, so they very much welcomed the suggestion.

At the beginning of our third week, I woke at 5 a.m. at camp 1 and thought about the next few days. In a few hours, we would set off for camp 2, hopefully arriving around 3 p.m.

We would have seven hours to rest up there and try to get some sleep. Then, at 10 p.m., we would set off for the summit push.

Our climbing guides had predicted it would take around fourteen hours to reach the summit of Himlung from camp 2. This would be a lengthy day, as we would try to make it all the way to the top without another camp to stay at. There would normally have been a camp 3 on a mountain of Himlung's size, but it couldn't be set up for various reasons so the summit push would have to begin from the lower camp.

Unzipping the tent, I left Arron to sleep and crawled out. It was slow progress and involved a fair amount of effort to unfold myself and get to my feet. The weight of the pack had caused stresses and strains I hadn't felt before. I had liked the idea of carrying my own pack up the mountain when we had initially decided to do this. There had been the financial constraints of hiring more guides to consider and summiting without someone else carrying my bag felt like what a proper mountaineer should do. But I was beginning to wonder if I should have made more allowances for my disability.

But the creaks and pains quickly dissolved as my eyes adjusted to the morning glow and my brain began to comprehend the scenery surrounding me. I will never become blasé about climbing out of a tent in the Himalayas. The air was entirely still and a feeling of serenity washed over me.

Across from us was another mountain on the Himlung range, with a gnarled rock face and glaciers topping it. As I stared towards it, an avalanche erupted on its south slope. Snow piled down its side, ice balls gathering pace, and it looked like the most inhospitable place on earth. It was a timely reminder not to let my guard down in a place that could inspire such calm.

I'd already witnessed several other avalanches on that same slope and the regularity with which they occurred suggested that a human had probably never set foot on it, due to the peril involved. With over eight billion of us now in existence and the increase of global travel, it is pretty rare nowadays to see a place that has never felt the pressure of a single footstep, but the Himlung Himal mountain range had a few in its folds. Beyond our camp, there weren't any signs of human life; there wasn't a single structure, telegraph pole or road. The sense of remoteness was invigorating, but I couldn't forget the vulnerability of our situation. We were truly alone.

When I returned to our camp, Kaji and Bigraj had made us porridge and a local sweet coffee that tasted as though it had more sugar in it than water.

'Are you not hungry?' I asked Ben, noticing his barely touched porridge in a metal bowl beside him.

'I just can't keep anything down,' he responded. 'I feel slightly nauseous all the time.'

'Just take it in slowly if possible, as you'll need the fuel later. Apart from that, how are you feeling?'

'I feel fine,' he said, picking up his bowl and forcing down a mouthful. 'I'm ready for this.'

We all were, because we had to be. We were about to follow the same route as the previous day but then continue through the icefall to camp 2, situated on a glacier at 6,030 metres. As we were getting higher up the mountain, we had to be constantly aware of the signs of altitude sickness as the air had less than fifty per cent of the oxygen it would have at sea level. All of us, including the guides, would soon feel its effects and headaches would become the norm. We had to watch out for them intensifying or becoming persistent as those were signs of altitude sickness, along with blurred vision, dizziness, vomiting, loss of appetite and hallucinations. I decided to keep an eye on Ben to ensure none of the other symptoms were creeping up on him.

To reduce the possibility of altitude sickness, we had to keep our packs as light as possible. Before leaving, we went through them again and ditched anything we didn't need for the summit push. Inside my tent, I made a small pile of some medical equipment, my toothbrush and toothpaste and a mid-layer. I was really down to the bare bones where every gram counted.

We stood outside for our last team photo before picking up our bags. As I swung my pack onto my back, I heard a huge crack that made me spin around. A ledge of ice had broken free from the mountain face I had been looking at earlier that morning. We watched in awe as it cascaded into the valley below. Another reminder of the mountains' power.

In a line, we trekked up the rocky mountainside towards the place we had stopped the day before. The sky was a clear, brilliant blue and we fell silent as we carefully picked our way upwards. As we walked, I enjoyed the final hours of the relative freedom my orthotic gave me to lift my left leg. I had been wearing my walking trainers rather than hiking boots the entire time as they worked better with my TurboMed, but it wouldn't be long until I switched to summit boots.

A few hours later, we could see the brilliant blue of the bottom of the icefall and we picked up our pace. When we arrived, I sat down next to Arron and took my orthotic and trainers off before pulling on the hulking summit boots and clipping on my crampons. Now that my left leg couldn't lift in the same way, I used my knee loop to pull my leg up and take the few short steps to a small cave where we all stashed our shoes. Walking without an orthotic was easier than I thought it would be, as my summit boots were so rigid they locked my foot into a right angle. It was a much better result than it pointing downwards, as my left foot would do without support.

'It is time to clip on,' Bigraj said, indicating the first fixed line to the boys.

Kaji was already linked to it and went first to show us how it was done. I craned my neck and stared up at the icefall. Imagine a twenty-metre-high, really irregular, ridiculously steep staircase made almost entirely from ice – that was what we would have to climb up to reach the next stage of our journey.

Although tricky to climb, icefalls are undoubtedly beautiful. They occur when a glacier runs over a steep section of rock; the corner of it will fragment and spill down as though a waterfall has been frozen in mid-motion. I watched as Kaji expertly kicked the front prongs of his right crampon into the ice and then stepped up, kicking the next crampon in and using his ice axe to steady himself. After the first ledge, he could walk up a steep curve and then he kicked his crampons in for the next small ledge. Up he went, making it look simple.

We were spaced out and I was the second-to-last to go up, with Shyam behind me. I kicked the crampon in on my right leg and hauled my left up with my arm, slowly making my way up the icefall. It would have been impossible without crampons – ingenious inventions that have transformed altitude mountaineering since the beginning of the twentieth century. They consist of a sheet of metal spikes that fit to the underside of a boot and dig into the snow or ice slopes to stop you from slipping. There are usually two spikes that point out from the toe that, if kicked in deeply enough, provide enough stability to create your own mini ledge that can take all of your weight. They help climbers scale sheer sheets of ice if necessary – a good thing for us, as towering walls of ice surrounded us. Fortunately for us, there were also regular small ledges and pathways up the icefall, so we only needed to use the front prongs for one or two steps at a time.

Halfway up, I looked down and felt the familiar whoosh of vertigo. Leo Houlding once told me that everyone is scared of heights and it was nice to know that most climbers weren't a superhuman breed of people impervious to the fear of falling. Instead, repeated exposure and confidence in their skills reduced it. I had learnt over the last couple of years that exposure therapy to heights really did help and I was now far more comfortable with them. However, my heart would still regularly race when I was high up, even though my brain would try and override the feeling with logic and a reminder of the rope I was attached to. When I reached the last ledge, I hauled my body up and Shyam helped me by lifting my left leg. We had done it.

I am never more alive than when I am in the mountains and, after the icefall, we encountered a situation that put me straight in the present moment. We had all gathered at the start of the second 150-foot-long fixed line. We were definitely now teetering on a 'high consequence' zone, as on the other side of the rope was a yawning chasm splintering deep into the ice – otherwise known as a crevasse. We were following a glacier and, where there were glaciers, there were usually also crevasses to contend with. Glaciers aren't stationary – those solid ice rivers slowly shifted down the mountainside, unable to resist the lure of gravity. The stress from the movement opened up crevasses – wedge-shaped cracks in the ice that were often deep enough to swallow a ten-storey building or more. I once saw a crevasse in Iceland that was so deep and wide that someone had flown a plane through it.

I clipped onto the line and moved up the rope slowly. My heart was pounding as there was just a single rope between me and the pitch-black abyss. Although the crampon for my left foot had been filed down as part of the adaptation for my kit, moving in crampons and heavier boots wasn't easy for me. The lack of power and lift meant I had to drag my leg a fair bit and all the time I was very aware that taking a tumble would have significant consequences. In moments like that, every cell in my body came alive and my nerves fizzed at the danger that lay so close to my feet. It was always an extraordinary sensation, almost raw in how close you were to death. Few people get to experience it – or even want to.

Once we got past the crevasse, we clipped onto the next stretch of 150-foot rope. Climbing an icefall and walking alongside a crevasse were the 'easy' bits for that day and it wasn't long before we reached the section the guides thought was such an anomaly they had already warned us about it. Up ahead, I spotted what had caused this worry. It was another crevasse, but this one was four feet wide and slashing its way across our path. We couldn't walk around it – we would have to leap over it. All around the crevasse, the snow was spiked into points like the jagged surface of a crampon.

As we were the first to climb Himlung in two years, the guides hadn't known that this 'exciting' new feature had formed. On more popular mountains, such as Everest, the

Nepalese government hire teams of climbing guides at the start of the season to fix the lines and strap ladders across the larger crevasses of this size. But Himlung was rarely climbed in comparison and therefore didn't justify that type of preparation. Perhaps by the mid-season on Himlung, word would spread that a ladder would be helpful, but right then we were ladderless and therefore expected to jump across the four-foot stretch. A ladder also wasn't technically necessary, as four feet would be considered a manageable size for most people with two working legs. But at least two people in our party would have given a lot for a few rungs of steel at that moment.

Beetle went first, balancing on the edge before leaping out and landing safely on the far side. Next up was Ben, whose crossing was a bit sketchier than Beetle's, but he got across safely. Then came my turn.

I slowly stepped towards the edge and couldn't resist peering down into the darkness. Even though the opening was only four feet, I could tell its depth was huge. I couldn't see where it ended, which left my imagination to fill in the gap. What it produced didn't exactly calm my nerves.

As I eyed up the width of the crevasse, I immediately knew I had an issue. Unlike most of our party, I couldn't jump, and four feet was at the absolute upper limit of my stride. Even if I did manage to get my good leg to step across, I didn't have the power to push off with my weaker left leg, so I could end up stuck straddling a crevasse – something that never had and never would feature high on my bucket list.

While I stood on the lip of the crevasse, holding the jumar for support, I tried to work out what to do. I thought back to the mantra I had developed on a holiday in New York following my accident. It was created when Lois and I had to take the subway while I was still in a wheelchair. I had decided the approach needed was 'just go for it'. That one saying had me crossing a foot-wide gap between the subway train and platform in a wheelchair, carried me onto small fishing boats in the Philippines and up a thousand stone stairs in Nepal. It had also brought me to the mountains. It taught me that if I always took the safe option with my disability, I would never get anywhere. On the other hand, I was very aware that the consequences were potentially very different when it came to the challenge ahead. A gaping crevasse would always jangle the nerves a little more than a misstep that might land me in the warm crystal waters of the Pacific.

But the simple fact was, there was only one way forward. I either had to cross the crevasse or turn around. It was time to just go for it.

Everyone gathered around the crevasse, wondering what I would do. Ben, Beetle, Bigraj and Kaji were on the other side, with Arron and Shyam behind me.

'Bigraj,' I said, while eyeing up the crevasse again. 'As soon as I take the step, I want you to pull hard on the rope attached to my harness. I'm hoping it will give me the momentum I need to make it over.'

Bigraj nodded and wound the rope around his arm.

'You've got enough slack,' Arron said from behind me as he straightened out the other end of the rope from my harness. 'I'll pull this side if you fall, so you don't go too deep.'

Everyone fell silent. I wasn't sure if I'd make it across and I was hoping the worst outcome would leave me dangling a few feet into the mouth of the crevasse on the rope I was attached to. Even though I kept on reminding myself of the rope, I was still terrified as a small part of my mind whispered, 'What if one of the ice screws gives way?'

I steadied myself on the lip of the crevasse with my left leg and took one last glimpse into the blackness. With a big pull of the jumar, I lunged for the other side.

Time stopped momentarily as I spanned the chasm, but with one well-judged pull from Bigraj, the rest of my body followed and I stumbled forward safely on the other side. There was nothing quite like a crevasse to get the old ticker going.

I sat down for a minute as an almost equally anxious Arron stepped forward and leapt over the crevasse. Even though he moved with ease, the dark slice below would test most people's nerve. Once we were all across, we rested for a few minutes, but soon it was time to follow the rest of the glacier up to camp 2. The next section looked just like the side of a mountain you would see in a film. It was a vast, steep slope covered in snow, but the guides had already told us there wouldn't be solid rock beneath our feet.

In the space of a few days, we had encountered three different types of glaciers, all with their own pitfalls. The land of the giants next to base camp had its unstable scree slopes, the icefall had its sheer heights, but the last type preferred to hide its dangers. When we think of glaciers, we probably think of them at the mountain base. But they usually start high up, where the ice has collected, and trace their way down to its base, taking the curved route of least resistance like a river would.

If you look at a photo of a mountain, a large proportion will be made up of glaciers that, to the untrained eye, look like rock covered in snow. But while you might sink into the snow with each step if you were to step onto a section of rocky mountainside, there would still be solid ground hidden underneath. The difference between this and a glacier is crucial, as glaciers present themselves as just part of the snow-covered mountainside but hide crevasses under a few inches or feet of snow. If the wind hasn't blown enough snow into the crevasse to fill it up, or the temperature isn't cold enough to freeze the snow in there, you could take a step onto what you thought was safe ground only to drop one or one hundred metres. It's the mountain's version of topographical Russian roulette.

The best chance we had was to follow the trail made the previous day by the climbing guides when fixing the lines, as they would have studied maps of where the glaciers were and their footsteps would be a good indicator of the solidity of the snow underneath. It was not the usual procedure to fix lines across this type of glacier, so instead we were attached to each other by one long rope in groups of three or four. Being tied to each other in this way meant that if someone fell down a crevasse, the body weight of the other two or three people would prevent them from falling too far. So, we spread out along the 150-foot rope and kept enough distance between us so we didn't accidentally tug at each other or get so close that we would both fall through the crevasse at the same time. We had a few kilometres of snow-covered glacier to trek up in this manner and I prayed the snow conditions would be compact enough for us to walk on its surface.

Unfortunately, we had no such luck. I walked behind Kaji and carefully tried to place my feet in the indents left by his footsteps, but with every step I sank lower than him as I was nearly a foot taller and carried a lot more weight. The snow was much softer than I had hoped, which meant I was sinking almost to my knees with each step. I quickly got into the zone of stepping with my right leg, leaning forward and then dragging my left leg so it could slide out of the hole and move forward. The process would then start again for the next step. More than a few times, I swore out loud at how soft the snow was. It was exhausting and I knew we would be in trouble if the temperature didn't drop over the next couple of days. None of us could continue like that up the rest of the mountain.

I stopped to pull the bottle of water from my bag and looked back at how the others were getting on. Below me, Ben was struggling. The fatigue had accentuated his foot drop and he was trying to pull his right leg out of the soft snow.

'God, I just wish my leg would work!' he shouted.

With a grunt, he gave a sharp tug on his leg but toppled to the side. He slid a few feet down the mountainside until Aaron's bodyweight prevented him from going any further. I knew how depressing it would be to have to wade through those few lost metres again.

'Are you okay?' I shouted to Ben.

'It's this snow,' he shouted back. 'I'm just sinking in it!'

I made my way down the few metres to him. He was lying on his back, his heavy rucksack pinning him down.

'It's impossible with a pack this heavy. Without this,' he said, pointing to his bag, 'I could do it.'

He sighed as he struggled to sit up. 'I feel like a turtle.'

He looked up at me, the exhaustion clear in his eyes as he tried to sit up again.

'Don't worry about it. Take some time if you need it.'

I was almost cross at Ben for being so tough on himself, so I tried to calm my voice in case he misinterpreted my tone.

'If you push yourself too hard, you'll make yourself ill. You're likely to get altitude sickness so let's just slow it down and go at a pace that is comfortable for you. Look, we're all more than happy to have a rest.'

Shyam came over and pulled Ben up to a seated position and I called for us all to have a ten-minute break. Ben sat with his head in his hands and, at that moment, I realized the chances of him making it to the top were slim. He was unwilling to admit how tired he was, but he couldn't keep exerting that amount of energy.

I sat next to him, but we didn't speak. It was always more testing when you were finding something difficult to be surrounded by people who didn't have the same mobility issues as you. You found yourself cursing the snow conditions, pack weight or anything else you could. I had experienced it too that day.

All too quickly, the break was over and we knew we had to continue the long trek across the glacier.

I kept checking on Ben and it was clear he was finding it much more challenging than the rest of us.

'My right leg has stopped working,' he told me when I dropped back to walk with him. 'I wish it would just work!'

At 3 p.m., six hours after leaving camp 1, we arrived at camp 2. We were all exhausted, but particularly me and Ben, as the deep snow had shown how much more difficult it was for someone with our injuries. When Ben and I were on solid surfaces and wearing orthotics, we could generally keep up with the others.

But that day had revealed the challenges we faced when we were unable to lift our legs properly. Our energy output had been extreme and as I slumped down outside my tent, I was already worried about the snow conditions on the next climb.

Camp 2 was on a rolling snow slope and a much less grand affair than camp 1. It comprised three orange tents huddled together and only their bright colours and the tracks leading to and from them marked the presence of human life on Himlung.

'I have a surprise for you all,' Beetle said, wandering over and holding his phone out.

I raised an eyebrow, unsure what Beetle had done for us.

'Come on,' he said, grinning. 'Don't you want to hear from Lois?'

Yes, I bloody well did. I followed him quickly into one of the tents. A few taps on his phone and there was Lois sitting next to my dog Baz, in a video message Beetle had secretly arranged for her to record before we left. 'I just wanted to wish you huge, huge good luck with climbing Himlung. Barry and I believe that you will get to the top of this mountain. But in all seriousness, it doesn't matter to me if you make it to the top. I am unbelievably proud to call you my husband. I'm so excited for our future together and I can't wait to get you back down the mountain and into my arms. I love you so much.'

It was exactly what I needed and I wandered outside the tent while Ben and Arron watched the messages Beetle had organized from their partners. Sitting outside, I marvelled at how I could see for miles. I had already forgotten about the view from camp 1 because, compared to what I was looking down at now, it paled in comparison. From my vantage point and with the clear sky, it felt like the whole of Nepal lay before me. Rows of snow-capped peaks stretched to the horizon to the south, while to the north, the upper slopes of Himlung Himal were now in full view. I tried to take it all in and appreciate the most epic view I had ever seen, but it was difficult and I soon found myself taking in the view from a horizontal position in my tent.

Lying on my side with the tent door open, I felt absolutely shattered and the fact we had to leave in a few hours for our summit push was playing on my mind. I couldn't comprehend how getting up and leaving camp 2 would be possible after one of my most challenging days in the mountains.

There was only one way to find out.

CHAPTER 11

Acceptance

Staring at the condensation freezing on the tent's roof, I was finding out the hard way just how difficult it was to sleep at 6,000 metres. At that height, the low oxygen levels meant waking up and gasping for air shortly after falling asleep. But I wasn't even being offered that opportunity. Instead, my head refused to allow me to fall asleep while it whirred in anticipation of what was to come. A mix of exhaustion and adrenaline created a knife-edge state within me, something I hadn't felt since I was on Mera Peak over two years ago. The same questions were repeated over and over in my mind. *What would the next few hours hold? How far would we get? Was this a good idea?*

The last question was a new one.

Arron groaned next to me. 'It's no good,' he said. 'I'm going to have to go outside and pee.'

I smiled. Peeing was where I had the upper hand in high-altitude climbing. While Arron went outside and risked literally freezing his nads off, I had my two-litre nighttime Conveen catheter, which meant I didn't need the nighttime scurries the other boys had to endure. When I'd told a few experienced mountaineers about this, they had been considering using one for future climbs rather than facing -15°C plus wind chill hitting their delicate areas.

We'd been zipped up in the tent for a couple of hours and the warmth from my Nalgene bottle was beginning to fade. These thick plastic containers were used as our water bottles during the day, but at night we would top them up with boiling water, wrap them in a sock and transform them into hot water bottles. Doing this also meant that when we woke in the morning, we would have water to drink that hadn't turned to ice, thanks to our body heat. As the climb progressed, we would even have to keep our water bottles next to our bodies during the day to stop them from freezing. Ben and I had to be careful with this type of hot water bottle as we had limited sensation and couldn't feel heat in certain areas of our bodies. Someone I know got third-degree burns on their stomach when their bottle slipped out of its sock and they couldn't feel it burning them throughout the night.

Soon, Arron returned, his teeth chattering.

'It's bloody freezing out there,' he said before clambering back into his sleeping bag.

We both lay there and the hours ticked by. While it had still been light, Arron had a dodgy tummy and had to speak to Shyam to ask if there was anywhere we could go to the toilet. He told Arron that because we were on a glacier, we'd have to be roped to him if we wanted to go for a number two. Arron had initially declined his offer as he didn't want to subject him to that level of proximity, but after half an hour of lying down in the tent, he decided he couldn't hold out. They roped up, levelled up their week-long friendship and wandered off together from the campsite. They returned a few minutes later as Arron popped his head back through the tent.

'I'm not sure Shyam appreciated that as much as I did,' he said with a smirk on his face.

I wasn't sure if Arron had fallen asleep after, but I was certain I didn't get a single minute of shut-eye. The repeating thoughts had started up again. *What would the next few hours hold? How far would we get? Was this a good idea?*

The alarm went off in my sleeping bag. Just like our water, anything electrical had to remain close to our body heat, otherwise it would die a quick death. My sleeping bag had become a bedside drawer with the amount of stuff I had stashed away in it. I thought of Beetle, whose sleeping bag must have been like a branch of Jessops with the camera equipment he had tucked up with him. Smiling, I rolled over and looked at Arron, who was staring at the tent's roof.

'Here we go,' I said.

He turned his gaze back to me and grinned. Judging by the lines under his eyes, he clearly hadn't got much sleep either. But none of that mattered now. It was all irrelevant because we had a mountain to climb.

I unplugged my night drainage bag from my catheter, attached my leg bag and zipped up my down trousers – all while still in my sleeping bag. We had gone way past the point of changing our pants as it was so cold no one could face the prospect of stripping off half their clothes and exposing themselves to the freezing temperatures, not to mention carrying the weight of extra pants as every gram counts when multiplied by thousands of steps at this altitude. It was 10 p.m. and the temperature outside was already nearly -20 °C. We also knew it was only heading in one direction this early in the night. This was why we were setting off so early: in the hope that the top layers of snow would be frozen and we wouldn't be descending in the heat of the day and falling through the glaciers.

Arron helped me put on my boots and gloves as my hands had seized up.

While he did this, I asked him to explain the Chinese philosophy of *wu wei* again. He had spoken about it the evening before while we all quickly ate, but I'd been tired and wasn't sure it had sunk in.

'It means "effortless action",' Arron said, while pulling on my left snow glove. 'It means to go with the flow and not resist life. It's about going with the season and nature and letting things happen in the right way. It's very easy when something happens to us to brace up, but then we don't make the right reactive decision about what happened. Whereas if you let it flow around you, there is less stress or strain on the body.'

'It's a bit like "control the controllable", then,' I said while holding out my curled right hand for him to put on my other glove.

'Control the controllable' is a philosophy I learnt from reading Viktor E. Frankl's *Man's Search for Meaning* in the early days of my recovery. Understanding that so many things were outside of my control after my accident eased my anxiety about my future, as I just focused on what was within my control: the small actions I could take towards my recovery and my overall mindset. Like 'effortless action', it doesn't mean sitting back and doing nothing. It just means stressing less about what comes your way. I had talked to Ben about it on our trek up to Himlung, but I wasn't sure whether he believed in it.

'Exactly. We can't control what comes in, but we can control how it comes out the other side. You've been practising *wu wei* for years already, Ed. You just didn't know the Chinese name for it.'

Arron unzipped the tent and crawled out before passing back my walking poles to me. Back on Mera Peak, my childhood friend, Rich, had helped me with these tasks when my hands clawed up from the cold and I lost all dexterity in them. Arron had gamely taken over this role without me even needing to ask. As I emerged from the last bit of shelter I'd see for a while, I was met by a blanket of stars so bright it almost felt like the sun hadn't set. I stared at them in awe until I heard the commotion coming from one of the tents behind me.

Kaji appeared from Ben and Beetle's tent with a concerned look.

'What's wrong?' I asked him.

'It is Ben. He is feeling dizzy and has been sick. He cannot continue.'

I trudged through the snow to Ben's tent and poked my head in. Beetle was already in his summit suit and kindly clambered out of the tent so I could sit with Ben. He was leaning up on his elbow with his eyes half closed and was clearly in a bad way.

'How are you feeling?' I asked.

'Pretty rough. Kaji said he thought it was the start of altitude sickness and I can't climb any further.'

'If Kaji says you can't go, you can't go. It's his call.'

'I know,' Ben said, looking up at the tent's roof. 'It's been a weird evening.'

I waited to see if he would elaborate and fortunately, he did.

'A few hours ago, I was at a crossroads. I'd gone outside to be sick while Beetle was asleep. After I threw up, I thought, *I could just cover the sick up with snow and no one would know.* I could have hidden it from you and forced myself up the mountain. A little devil was sitting on my shoulder, telling me to cover it up and that I could still make it to the top.'

'What changed your mind?' I asked, softly. My voice had been much lower for the past few days due to dehydration drying up my vocal cords.

'On the other shoulder was an angel telling me if I did that and something happened to me further up, I'd jeopardize everyone's climb and it would be my fault they didn't make it to the summit. Even if I forced myself up there, I couldn't live with myself if I did that.'

I nodded. Ben had put us ahead of his dream to summit Himlung.

'I'm really proud of what you've achieved, Ben. You're still the second person in history to get over 6,000 metres with our type of injuries and you put in a shift to get there.' I grinned. 'And you'd only climbed Ben Nevis before. That's nuts when you think about it.'

Ben's eyes lit up when he thought about it that way. 'Yeah, I'm proud of what I've achieved too. Yesterday was the toughest day for me. Every time I put my foot down, it just sank further, and as I tried to get myself back up, my foot would go even deeper. It took everything out of me.'

'You've made the right decision by not trying to hide your altitude sickness. Besides, you've got a big chunk of sick in your beard still, which is a bit of a giveaway.'

'The last couple of hours, it just clicked in my head that the journey makes the trip, not the summit. Don't get me wrong, it would have been nice to get to the top,' Ben said, before grinning. 'Especially if you all get up there.'

I smiled back at him. A week ago, I wouldn't have even hoped for Ben's level of acceptance of his situation. He'd finally realized he didn't have anything to prove. Rather than looking at what he couldn't do, he was looking at what he could do.

'How are you feeling about the summit push?' Ben asked.

'I'd be lying if I said there wasn't much adrenaline rushing around,' I responded, shoving my hands further into my down jacket to try and get them working again. 'I think I'm just going to see how far we get. Honestly, I'm just relieved you've taken turning around so well. I've been worried about you.'

'I'm alright, you don't need to worry about me. I've decided to go with the flow a bit more and try only to control the controllable.' He grinned at me. That was what I had been advising him for weeks, but I hadn't thought it had landed. 'I've got a lot to go back to in the UK. Kaji said I should stay here until it gets light and then he'll take me back down to camp 1 and then to base camp. So, I'll see you in a couple of days.'

He was already slumping back into his sleeping bag, the exhaustion finally claiming him for the night. 'Good luck, mate,' he said, his eyes closing.

I smiled. 'Thanks, and yes, see you in a couple of days.'

We said our goodbyes to Kaji, roped up and headed off into the unknown behind our new lead guide, Shyam. I set off into the night with a smile on my face due in part to Ben's sensible decision to stop there, but mainly his acceptance of it. He had finally begun to normalize what had happened to him after jumping out of that plane and he was now accepting the new version of himself. Yes, the pre-accident Ben might have been able to get past camp 2, but equally, he might not have done.

He might also have had altitude sickness and had to return down the mountain. Either way, it didn't matter and had never mattered. Ben would now be returning to the UK after having had the headspace to adjust. He was no longer comparing what the Ben before his accident could do to the one afterwards. In those few weeks in Nepal, Ben had finally grappled with the frustration of not being the person he was before. I knew from my own experience that it was hard to let go of that person. But once you accepted they had gone, you could begin to rebuild your life. All the worries that had been building over the last couple of weeks about Ben had dissipated and if there could have been a spring in my step with giant summit boots on, there would have been.

Arron and Beetle were both in their summit suits now and Arron's was a fetching bright green colour. They made everyone look a bit like Teletubbies but were incredibly lightweight, considering the bulk of insulation they provided. I had decided not to wear a summit suit – not for fashion reasons, but because of my difficulties regulating my temperature. Instead, I had a thick jacket over the top of down-filled salopettes. A lot of planning had gone into the kit element of the trip and, after discussing it at length with Berghaus, we thought it best if I had the option to take a layer off if necessary. My temperature regulation was irregular at best after my spinal cord injury – overheating was a real issue given that I couldn't sweat below the chest line anymore. At lower altitudes, we combated this by adding extra ventilation zips to the shoulders and upper back of my jacket. That wasn't possible with thick down, so I needed to be able to take it off, which would have been a bit tricky if I had been wearing a giant babygrow like the others.

The first stage of the climb was to traverse across a broad ridge towards where camp 3 would have usually been. From there, we would start the 1,200-metre vertical slog to the summit. Although my legs felt heavy, and there was the usual dragging of my left crampon through the snow, things felt good underfoot. The freeze we had hoped for had happened, so apart from the odd deep step, we were pretty much walking over the top of the snow, which made for decent progress. The light from my headlamp highlighted my summit boots, which I was mostly staring down at to ensure I placed my feet in Arron's footprints to try and conserve as much energy as possible. However, whenever I did have the chance to look up, the silvery light from the moon and stars reflected off the snow and opened up all of Himlung's mountain range to me. I could see almost as far as I would in the daylight, but everything had been stripped of colour. It was like walking in an eclipse of neither night nor day.

After around half an hour, we made it onto the ridge that we would have to walk along to where camp 3 would have been. The ridge was the safest route to the top but it meant we would be walking for a few hours without gaining any vertical metres, as we would be travelling across the mountain rather than up it.

'Good snow conditions, eh?' Bigraj said from behind me.

I could hear from his voice that he was smiling.

'Yes, mate,' I responded. 'Couldn't have asked for better.'

My hopes and energy levels were high and I started thinking we might have a good chance of making it to the summit if it continued like this.

'I hope it stays like this for the Kenyans,' Bigraj added.

The Kenyan team was a day behind us and it had been agreed

that we would attempt to summit before them so we wouldn't hold each other up on any of the fixed lines. That night, they would be sleeping at camp 1 before making their way up to camp 2 in the morning. They would probably pass Ben when he was making his way down.

I'd borrowed the down jacket I was wearing for the summit from Leo Houlding, who'd had it made for one of his Antarctic expeditions, so I was certain it would keep me warm enough when needed. It wasn't long before I felt the first bead of sweat forming on my forehead and the jacket soon found its way into Arron's bag. It might seem a bit strange taking off a coat at around -15 °C, but there was no wind chill on the ridge and in those conditions, combined with how hard I was having to work by the second hour, I was finding it plenty warm enough.

Arron and I would stop and have a few sips of the water he was carrying for both of us every half an hour or so. Some of the bottles were filled with water mixed with electrolytes to replenish the salts we would lose while sweating. We had measured out enough water to get us to the summit and back as we didn't want so much so that it would weigh us down, but we also didn't want to run out. It was a fine balance where the ideal outcome would be that we were taking our final sips just as we returned to camp 2. We knew we'd probably be quite dehydrated even if we were taking our last drink then, but as long as it wasn't too severe, we would be alright. This was far preferable to returning to camp 2 with loads of full water bottles as we would have wasted so much energy carrying them.

As we trudged along the ridge, I began to think about Lois and how much I wished she could see some of the views of Nepal. But even though I wanted her to be there with me,

I also knew she would bloody hate sleeping in a tent and eating the same food over and over again. That was not her idea of something fun to do with your spare time. But I knew she'd appreciate the scenery just as much as I did – she would probably just want to be airlifted in to see it. Fair play to her; forgoing washing and sleep was not everyone's cup of tea.

Someone who I knew would appreciate it, warts and all, was my childhood friend Tom. He was the one who had spurred me and Rich on to try new things, some of which we joined in with and some we said a hard no to. I later wished we had said yes to more of what Tom had suggested, because he was taken from us at the age of twenty-three and I would never hear one of his madcap ideas again. I would have given a lot to see Tom bounce up to us, a grin on his face, his thoughts going a hundred miles an hour as his mouth tried to keep up. When he died, I thought I would never get over it. And I never did. I just got through it and it was going through the experience of losing Tom that was one of the main reasons I was able to face the repercussions of my accident.

I had been thinking a lot over the last couple of weeks about my life's direction and I could see two paths before me. Since I'd been doing TV work, presenting the rugby and the Paralympics, which I loved, more roles had been coming in. I'd been incredibly grateful for these additional opportunities, but I also knew that if I accepted them, I would have less time working with the beneficiaries of my charity and also less time in the mountains. I was torn. Most people would think I was crazy to turn down additional work and it was always in the back of my mind that I wanted to lessen any financial constraints on Lois as she worked really hard in our charity and was earning less money from it as the CEO than some of the employees. It all came down to pursuing what I was passionate about versus being financially sensible. What I had figured out, too, was that for the past five years, I'd always said yes to what I was passionate about and we hadn't done too badly. Logically, there was nothing to indicate it wouldn't continue. Pleased I had finally made up my mind about this, I stopped and treated myself to a swig of water before setting off again.

Two hours in, the snow gave way beneath me and I plummeted into my first crevasse.

CHAPTER 12

Digging In

All it had taken was one simple step and my legs had disappeared through the snow. I was up to my waist and the feeling of nothing but air beneath my feet was terrifying. I looked down and there was just black beneath me, no indication of how far I would have fallen if the rope hadn't caught me. Fortunately, my yelp of surprise and the tug of the rope had alerted everyone to what had happened.

'Are you okay, Ed?' Arron yelled, along with similar calls for reassurance from the rest of the team.

'Umm, I suppose so,' I shouted, grateful I hadn't dropped further.

We had trained for how to deal with crevasses and the most important thing was what you do before you fall into the crevasse rather than afterwards. As long as we all walked with the rope 'kissing the surface' so there was some slack between us, we wouldn't fall too far or jolt our teammate into potentially toppling over too.

Beetle and Arron leant back and pulled the rope tight to prevent me from falling further while Bigraj and Shyam tried to help pull me out. I reached forward with my ice axe to try and get some purchase to pull myself higher. I was pretty deep in there and didn't have much strength or energy after what we'd been through over the previous few days. I pulled myself forward, groaning with the strain. Half of my right leg was out before my ice axe dislodged and I slid back down again. I leant my head on the snow, exhausted. Nothing was worse than battling to move forward and then sliding backwards; all that energy was wasted and more was required to return to where you had been only a few seconds ago.

After ten minutes of pulling and wiggling, I crawled out on my stomach and freed my legs. My heart was racing and I just lay there for a moment. Eventually, I slowly got to my feet and looked down at the hole I'd left in the path. At least the Kenyans would now know not to step there.

I took ten more steps and felt the snow give way beneath my foot – another crevasse. Already tired from pulling myself out of the first one, I had to start the whole procedure again. The ropes tightened and I wriggled and ice-axed myself out of it before getting to my feet again. *Bloody crevasses*, I thought.

The ridge we were walking along was the glacier's pathway down the mountain. The snow was hard and I had been stepping in Shyam's footsteps, so I thought I was safe. The snow bridges had taken the weight of the Nepalese guide, but they were crumbling under my larger frame. It proved you can't ever let your guard drop high on the mountains.

As I fell down my third, then fourth crevasse, I thought back to the meal we had shared in the mangrove restaurant, where Bigraj and I had referred to Himlung as a 'stepping stone'. Some stepping stone. We had certainly stepped a bit further than any of us had imagined. But that was the way with mountains. With all the planning in the world, they were still in control and could brush you aside just as easily as if you were an unwelcome gnat.

We continued slowly along the ridge line, conscious that, at any point, we could be walking over a crevasse without knowing it. Every time one of us fell down one, we all had to stop so they could get out. We were losing so much time and our pace was already glacial. Since leaving camp 2, we hadn't gained any vertical metres and I was growing increasingly concerned about our lack of progress. No one spoke unless it was to give instructions on how to help someone who had fallen. We were too tired for conversation and had each retreated within ourselves so we could focus on not falling and the simple act of breathing.

It was still dark at 4 a.m. when we reached the site where camp 3 should have been. A few tent poles sticking up cast a skeletal shadow across the snow. It was in quite a precarious position with a high drop to its far side and a steep slope in front of it. No one had been there for two years and it had been swallowed up and destroyed by the mountain.

We stopped for a ten-minute break and I decided to sit down despite being uncertain whether letting my body rest was a good idea. After five hours of crossing a ridge filled with crevasses, I didn't know how much more I had left in me. As I stared out at the decimation of camp 3, it began to look quite appealing as I imagined it with three taut orange tents with down sleeping bags tucked inside. I started to think about the difference it would have made to cut six hours off the summit push and the recovery time we would have had there. But we could do nothing about it now, so I quickly checked myself. Thoughts like that wouldn't help me as the situation was outside of my control and I knew to focus solely on what was *within* my control, just as I had learnt to do after my accident. In this case, that was food and water. I ate as much as my dry mouth could bear, the energy bar catching in my throat, and then pushed myself wearily to my feet to set off again.

I knew from an earlier briefing that camp 3 was close to where we would start climbing upwards and sure enough, it wasn't long before we reached the first fixed line that headed steeply up into the darkness. It was a welcome sight as it meant that once we attached ourselves to it, there was a minimal chance of us disappearing off the side of the mountain. It also meant we were on the correct route and hadn't grown disorientated after tackling the crevasses. There were so many mountaineering horror stories of climbers getting disorientated in the altitude and wandering off in the wrong direction. Most of them didn't end well for the people involved.

We unroped from each other and Beetle set off first up the fixed line, making slow and steady progress with the jumar. It was impressive how well he had taken to life in the Nepalese mountains, considering this was the first time he had climbed anything outside of Scotland.

It was my turn next and I clipped my carabiner to the rope, which would stop me from falling down the mountainside, and grabbed the jumar, which would make ascending the rope easier. I folded one pole, handed it to Bigraj, and started to haul myself up the line with a pole in the other hand to steady myself.

To say it was hard work would be the understatement of the century. Even though I had the jumar and rope, the increase in gradient from the ridge was pronounced. Gravity was constantly pulling me backwards, while my body was trying to do everything to battle against it. I quickly realized that my left leg had given up due to exhaustion – it was now just a passenger, leaving my right leg and arm to do the work to lift myself and my left leg up the mountain. The lack of oxygen made itself known again. I was gasping for breath because of how much was needed. One step at a time, I pulled myself up. On the fifth step, I kneeled and rested my head on the freezing snow to try to catch my breath. My chest was tight and I couldn't believe how determined the mountain was to beat me.

I felt weak, which was not something I was used to. I scanned the past few days for an anomaly that had created this. After a while, I realized it was probably an accumulation of events rather than a single one.

I stood, not ready to give up, and took another five steps before folding down on the snow again. If I had teleported in, fresh from the airport, this would have been a different story – apart from passing out from the shock of the altitude change. But I wasn't fresh from the airport. I had done two weeks of hiking and then climbed two thousand vertical metres on only a few hours of sleep. The amount of energy expended to reach that point meant I was running at about twenty per cent of my full capacity, at altitude, dehydrated, using one leg. With every hour that ticked by, I was weakening. As I lay with my forehead resting on the snow, my next five steps completed and my left leg totally numb, I thought about how the most challenging thing with high-altitude mountaineering is that you did the most demanding part at the end, when you were at your weakest. Combine this with the altitude – which makes your heart beat faster and your metabolism speed up, while suppressing your appetite and dehydrating you – and climbing a forty-degree slope was like running an entirely uphill marathon with a 10 kg backpack on, having done a couple of marathons earlier in the week.

Another five steps. I occupied my mind by thinking about the journalists who interviewed me after I climbed the height of Everest on the staircase at my dad and stepmum's house during lockdown. Several of them asked me, 'Now you've done the height of Everest, are you going to do the real thing?' I smiled to myself in the dark and wished they could see me now. They clearly had no idea about mountains. When I climbed Everest's height on some stairs, I had a fridge at the bottom and a bed at the top. There were rails on either side of the staircase and I went from six metres above sea level to nine. The real thing was an entirely different matter.

Ten minutes later, Beetle shouted down to me, but I was so far into my thoughts that my brain hadn't registered his words.

'What did you say?' I shouted back up, my voice hoarse.

'I've reached the top of the line and the next bit is flattened out.'

I looked up to see his head torch glowing back down at me from about thirty metres away. Thank God for that.

We were about 6,150 metres high and real doubt came into my mind for the first time about whether I would make it to the top. We had been going for seven hours, hadn't slept in twenty-four and still had another 900 vertical metres to go. My right leg was exhausted because my left side had all but stopped working and the jumaring was proving more energy-sapping than expected.

Whenever I do these endurance tests, I am used to the constant internal monologue at challenging moments. I know from experience my brain will try to make me stop before my body is done. It's a protection mechanism in all of us and I've learnt to silence that chatter and push past that point, as it is the only way for me to get close to my true limits. I thought I knew how to push myself before my accident, whether it was running fitness tests in pre-season or digging in for the last ten minutes of a tough game, but I had no idea. You don't know where those limits lie until your back is against the wall. I had redefined my psychological limitations through those dark days following my accident, when I had to keep trying to wiggle a toe to learn how to walk again. I was in one of those moments again and I wasn't going to let the voice in my head tell me what to do. I had to dig in and get on with it. A battle had to commence and I pulled myself up from the snow to face it.

The thirty metres up to Beetle felt like it took a lifetime. My lungs and legs were on fire when I eventually unclipped and slumped down beside him. I looked back along our route and could see the distant shapes of our tents at camp 2. I thought of Ben and hoped he was okay. It wouldn't be long until he would be getting up to head back down the mountain. It was 5.30 a.m., and the light had started to change in the distance. The huge, shadowed outlines of the Himalayan giants stretched as far as the eye could see. Those mountains had proved yet again how savage they were. But, my god, they were beautiful as the sky changed colour in the dawn light.

CHAPTER 13

Summiting

It wasn't long until, one by one, Arron, Bigraj and Shyam unclipped from the fixed line and sat next to me. It was nice to know I wasn't the only one in our party gasping for air after the steep pitch. Thankfully, we had reached the final flat section before the relentless forty-degree slope to the summit began – all 900 vertical metres of it. We had a drink and ate some energy bars, which I tried to think of as 'breakfast', before roping ourselves together.

'How are you doing, mate?' Arron asked me as he secured the carabiner attached to his harness.

'Hanging in there,' I replied.

He smiled and patted my shoulder. 'Me too, fella. But we're still here, aren't we?'

Arron was right. The mountain hadn't defeated us, even though it had tried pretty hard to. I turned and stared up at the looming shadow of the upper reaches of Himlung and then did the only thing I could do – put one foot in front of the other.

As we trudged along the last piece of flat ground we would see for a while, I began to notice the sky changing colour again. The blacks had given way to deep blues, with a hint of orange growing on the distant horizon. Despite the sky's developing palette, the majority of my time was spent staring at my feet so I could place them in the impressions left in the snow ahead of me. At this stage, missing the footprint in front of me could add another minute or two to each step. On the rare occasion I did have the chance and the energy to look up, not only had the painting above me changed, but I was hit by a wave of awe all over again.

The next time I glanced upwards, the awe was accompanied by an audible gasp. We had reached the lip of the slope and had found ourselves staring north over Tibet, a view we hadn't encountered until this point as the mountain range had been blocking it. It was breathtaking. Rocky peaks and shimmering lakes spread like a crumpled quilt towards the Tibetan plateau. The glow of the sunrise to the east was lighting up the higher summits, like beacons guiding the giants on the other side of the Himalayas. Once again, I felt like a Borrower who had wandered into another realm.

At that moment, I had an overwhelming understanding that all of my efforts, not just over the last few weeks but over the past few years, had been worth it to arrive at that moment, to see and feel what was before me. I turned to the others, who were also standing with their mouths open. If we weren't so dehydrated, there may have been a few tears. Overwhelming beauty mixed with exhaustion was a powerful combination.

It was Bigraj who spoke first. 'We need to keep moving.'

Of course, he was right, but it was with a great deal of reluctance that I pulled myself away. I could have stayed forever, but it was nearing 7 a.m. and we were slipping behind our schedule. The long ascent to the summit was now fully visible in front of us, with the fixed lines heading off into the distance. It was an amazing feeling to be the only people on that huge, beautiful mountain, a feeling that justified the effort and distance to get there. But all of that diminished as I clipped onto the first fixed line and pulled my passenger leg with me. There were no more hidden sections or explanations of what came next from our guides. It was there for us to see – 900 vertical metres of pure, grinding slog.

Beetle went first so he could capture the uninterrupted views for his footage and then it was Shyam, with me following. Behind me was Arron, with Bigraj bringing up the rear. I stepped with my right leg into Shyam's footprint, slid the jumar to meet it, and used the rope to pull myself and my passenger leg up with it. If my left leg got stuck, I would physically haul it up. The going was tough, but I was pleased to be able to take ten steps before resting, unlike the previous fixed line where I had limited myself to five. There was hope for summiting if I could keep up that pace.

Half an hour later, the strain was too much. I had to reduce to five steps before stopping to catch my breath. Then, with some dismay, I cut it back to three steps twenty minutes later. The gradient still meant I couldn't swing my left leg through, so I had to use my right leg first and then drag the other to meet it, rather than being able to place it ahead. Although functional, my right leg had no pain sensation, which worked in my favour in these situations. I didn't feel the usual burning of lactic acid buildup, which allowed me to push it much further than I otherwise could. The downside in this scenario, where I was pushing myself to the brink, was there was no way to gauge my leg's fatigue other than by seeing if it was still working. It didn't take long for my right leg to send me clear messages about its functionality. After an hour on the fixed line, it wasn't able to take many steps before it refused to respond to my commands and I was forced to give it time to recover.

After another hour of this, we reached our first obstacle. Beetle had stopped in front of a crevasse dissecting the path, with a similar one further along.

'What should I do?' Beetle asked as he waited for Shyam to catch up with him.

It was the first time any of us had spoken in an hour.

'There is no way around,' Shyam said. 'I checked when I fixed the lines. We have to step over them.'

Fortunately, they weren't as wide as the four-foot monster we had previously faced. Given the limited power output I had, combined with the gradient, I didn't think I would be able to tackle one that wide again. It still made for quite an intimidating challenge and as I lined up in front of the crevasse, I decided that, yet again, I would just have to go for it. As I eyed up the two-foot gap, I decided to take the unconventional approach of diving forward while pulling on the jumar at the same time. I fully expected to land on my face but managed to stay upright. It wasn't pretty, but it worked. The next crevasse was similarly tackled.

Time began to slip away from me. There was nothing to break up the relentless tunnel I had fallen into of staring at my feet and trying to get my right leg to work. I eventually stopped to check my watch as I had no idea if thirty minutes or three hours had passed. It was 11 a.m. This meant we had left camp 2 just over twelve hours before and I had been awake for thirty. There was nothing to do but carry on.

The grind was very real. All conversation had stopped

between us and I could tell Arron was digging in as well, as he was also just staring at his feet with little time for the view.

New depths of exhaustion were hitting me and my left leg was beginning to spasm with nearly every step. I was down to one movement at a time – a leg lifted or a slide of the jumar – with a break between each one. Tired to my bones, I turned around and sat down on the slope, digging my crampons in so as not to slide. Even resting was hard work; the gradient meant my legs had to remain under constant tension to keep me from sliding down the mountain and I could feel my quads juddering with the strain.

I stared down at Arron below me and then turned to look at the summit. My oxygen-deprived brain brightened when I realized it didn't look too far. At the same time, a voice of reason reminded me that distances could be deceiving in those landscapes. Scale is so hard to judge without any landmarks and only a blanket of white to try and glean information from.

'How high are we?' I asked Shyam, my voice croaky.

He checked his watch. 'Just above 6,700 metres.'

I couldn't believe it. We had covered around 500 vertical metres and were over halfway with another 400 to go. The last few hours had been a blur. Without realizing it, I had climbed well past the previous spinal cord injury record, which I had previously set. It was the highest I had ever been on foot. There was a brief feeling of relief, combined with pride, that I had beaten my record in terms of vertical metres. But every mountain is different and requires varying levels of effort. I knew that just by getting to camp 1 on Himlung, given its remoteness and the weight of the backpack I had been carrying, I had physically achieved much more than when I had summited the 6,500 metres of Mera Peak. Despite this, it was still nice to know we were now in new territory, in terms of altitude, for what someone with my type of injury could achieve.

I looked upwards. Only 400 vertical metres stood between us and the summit. The problem was that the last 500 vertical metres had taken us five hours and now we were in even thinner air and with much less energy. I stared at the summit one last time and dragged myself to my feet.

'Just keep stepping,' I said to myself.

I pulled hard on the jumar while pushing off with my right leg; the crampon on my left scraped through the ice as I dragged one foot to meet the other. I then tried to move my right leg forward. Nothing happened. I tried again, but nothing.

The signals my brain was sending were not reaching their destination, just like after I dived into the pool all those years ago. I slumped down onto all fours and stretched my right leg out behind me to let it rest, internally pleading with it to start working again.

As I crouched there on the snow, Bigraj passed Arron and kneeled next to me.

'I have some oxygen,' he said, holding the small canister to my face. 'It will help.'

I shook my head, too tired to speak. I didn't want any oxygen, even though I knew how much it would help.

I had read a lot around mountaineering and had many conversations with experienced mountaineers and listened to their varied opinions towards oxygen while mountaineering. Many saw it as a way for less experienced climbers to scale heights they wouldn't otherwise have a chance of reaching and it is one of the most heated debates in the community, seen by some as a quick fix akin to doping. In late 2020, there was a huge controversy in relation to the first winter ascent of K2, where using oxygen was compared to doing the Tour de France on an electric bike. Without a doubt, scaling a peak without oxygen was seen as more prestigious, as was tackling a new route that no one had done before or climbing unassisted without guides fixing lines or porters carrying luggage. Some people would even go as far as saying that using oxygen, fixed lines or porters meant you hadn't reached the height you thought you had achieved.

I have never felt I had anything to prove to anyone other than myself. I'm not in competition with other climbers because of my disability. I'm unique, in my own situation. Everyone's approach was different, but in my mind, I wanted to climb mountains in a safe, independent, pure way. I don't have any issues with people using oxygen when they are going to 8,000 metres – few can climb in what is known as the 'Death Zone' without it. But I didn't want to use it on Himlung. In my mind, I was determined that if I was going to scale 7,000 metres, I would do it without oxygen or not do it at all.

After a minute or so of stretching my leg, I dragged myself back to my feet to dig in again. How long could I keep going? I didn't know, but I wanted to find out. I moved my right leg forward, stopped to rest, and then dragged my left leg forward.

I repeated this process with all my effort over and over again until about an hour later, I stopped on all fours. Pain spiked through my body and my legs and arms were shaking. I just wanted to hug them into me. My mind was so fragile it was humming and buzzing like it was about to go offline. I was at breaking point but knew I had to just keep on putting one foot in front of the other. I just needed to get my damn leg working again.

Then, deep within me, a feeling, a knowing, bubbled in my chest before spreading to my limbs and mind. It was an overwhelming understanding that this was as far as I should go. At first, I thought it was a new trick 'The Bin' was playing on me.

I lifted my head and gasped. It felt as though a literal force was pulling me back down the mountain and I dug my crampons in to prevent myself from sliding backwards. I had never felt anything like it before. I instantly knew it would be foolish and potentially perilous to ignore it. Something or somewhere had granted me the knowledge that if we didn't turn around, someone might die as a consequence of that decision. Not right then, as we were still safe, but in a few hours when the sun went down.

'My body won't let me do anymore,' I said, my voice breaking.

Arron was a few metres back, head down, battling hard to reach me but having to take a short break every couple of steps as he was carrying our supplies. About twenty metres ahead, Beetle crouched on his haunches, looking down at us and breathing heavily. Behind him was the summit, so tantalizingly close.

I was in shock at the situation and didn't know what to do. Yes, of course, I hadn't reached the top of mountains before – that's part of the game – but every time before, the decision had been taken out of my hands, whether it was down to bad weather, Covid-19 or even dodgy paperwork. But I had never consciously decided to turn around. Crouching there, I couldn't remember a single instance in my life where I had given up on anything. It's not in my nature, particularly when I can see the finish line.

The younger me might have pushed on for a further 200 vertical metres, determined to say he had reached 7,000 metres even if he couldn't reach the 7,150 summit of Himlung. He might have done it because to go from heights beginning with a six to ones starting with a seven would mean reaching another clear point in his climbing achievements. My younger self's ego might have pushed us further up that mountain. No one would have stopped me, as everyone was loyal to me and my dream, but one or more of us could end up dying on a mountainside.

I wasn't my younger self anymore. Like Ben, I also had a life to return to in the UK. Lois was waiting for me, probably thinking about me at that very moment, wondering how I was getting on. Would she tell me to turn around or continue? Despite having always surrounded myself with people who helped me push myself further – Lois included – I knew the answer immediately. I had seen it with other mountaineers and people who are into extreme sports. Once they had a partner they loved, or children, they knew there was something more important to them than the next achievement. One false move could claim a life, so they reined it back in, even if it was subconsciously.

I also had some insight into what life-changing accidents do to those you love. The effects rippled outwards; not only did your life dramatically alter, but so did the lives of those closest to you. In the early days following my accident, after I had been moments from death in an ambulance, it was like I was experiencing my own funeral. People flew in from other countries to visit me, people told me things they had been meaning to say for years and Lois, in a moment of pure grief, shouted out that she had always wanted children with me. I realized how loved I was, and by so many people. I couldn't put them all through that again. Last time, I made a split-second decision and nearly died. This time, I had been granted the chance to consider my options and I knew I didn't want to die as a consequence of them.

I slumped forward, my head in my hands, and found myself sobbing into the snow, my mind exhausted and broken.

I wasn't sad. Every cell in my body told me the right decision was to turn around. For the first time in my life, I had found my limit. It felt monumental to meet it, finally, after a lifetime of pushing myself further and further beyond what even I thought I was capable of. I wondered if it would have been better to leave those things unknown. To always have some untapped part of you waiting in the wings.

There were reasons why we hadn't been able to summit, including being the first people up the mountain in two years, no high camp, the snow conditions being so poor and not knowing what to expect. None of that changed the fact that if it weren't for me, the people around me wouldn't have been there. That was an enormous sense of responsibility and it was one the altitude hadn't stripped me of – yet. But it could do. Summit fever has claimed many a life and will claim many more. My life was one thing, but the lives of my friends were another. The mountain was telling me to go down and that if I didn't, we would pay the price.

I turned my head to Arron, who was kneeling beside me. 'That's it, mate. I have to turn around.'

'Okay, let's go,' he said while trying to calm his own breathing.

'You don't have to come with me. I can start heading down with Shyam by myself.'

'No way,' he said. 'I'm done. It's time.'

We were at 6,800 metres and I knew my attempt to summit Himlung was over.

But at that altitude, my mind had quietly swept away the knowledge that the trouble usually begins on the descent.

CHAPTER 14

What Goes Up . . .

I raised my head and glanced down the mountain. Bigraj
was still kneeling beside me, holding the oxygen tank he had
removed from his pack.

I stared at it, wondering what it would allow me to do.

'Do you want?' he asked, bringing it closer.

I considered it again for a second. Maybe if I used oxygen,
I could carry on a bit further.

The tug of gravity pulled at me. Down the mountain it
wanted me to go. It was an overwhelming physical sensation
I couldn't ignore – as though the mountain was telling me
I couldn't go any further.

The crunch of crampons on ice let me know Beetle had
joined us from above.

I looked up, unsure how to tell him. He was here because of
me and I was the one who wasn't going any further.

'I'm done, Beetle. I'm turning around.'

He knelt and patted my shoulder. 'You've given it everything,
Ed. No one could say otherwise.'

That was undoubtedly true. I got off my knees and shuffled
around to face the descent. It was a start in the right direction.
We would have to get moving soon, as we had minimal food

and water and the last thing we wanted was to descend at night in our condition and with the crevasses we would have to cross.

I turned to Beetle. 'How are you feeling?'

He smiled. 'I'm absolutely fucked, mate, if I'm honest. But I think I've still got some left in me.'

I nodded, a decision already forming in my mind. 'You and Bigraj should carry on. You're both a lot quicker, so you will probably catch up with us on the descent.'

I wanted nothing more than for him to continue rather than forever wondering whether he could have summited. That sort of thing can stay with a person. He turned and stared up at the peak, then back to Bigraj, who I knew would take good care of him. I could tell he was torn.

'Go on if you want,' I said. 'If you're feeling okay, give it a good crack. But don't do anything silly. The mountain isn't going anywhere.

'Are you sure?'

'Absolutely. We'll see you further down.'

Beetle turned to Bigraj. 'Are you up for it?'

Bigraj grinned. 'Let's do this.'

They both stood and with loud shouts of 'Good luck!' following them, took their jumars in their hands and set off up the fixed line. I watched them for five minutes as they continued the periodic step count, hoping they would make it to the top. But for now, I had to concentrate on making it to the bottom.

It was 2 p.m., fifteen hours since we had left camp 2 and thirty-three hours since I had last slept. My body had very little left to give and we had hardly any supplies to replenish it. But we had to get down the mountain and I was relieved that at least down would be easier than up. Many mountaineers found descents more physically challenging than ascents because the consequences of falling down the slope were more severe than falling into it and you would have already accumulated so much fatigue on the ascent. But my legs functioned so much better going downhill as my extensor muscles – the ones that helped straighten a limb – worked better than my flexor muscles, which allowed you to bend a limb. You needed flexors to go up and extensors to go down. Combined with now having a full leg swing, I was confident I could pick up my pace.

I pushed myself to my feet as I knew Arron and Shyam were waiting for me to signal I was ready. Enjoying the ability to swing my right leg fully, I put my weight onto it.

It only took one step to realize I was in big trouble.

My good leg had all but given up and felt like it could collapse at any moment. I kept this to myself as I dragged my left leg to meet it. All the while, my brain was searching for why this had become so difficult. It wasn't supposed to be like that. I should have been able to power down the slope. I then realized that the eccentric contractions in my quads, where the muscle was lengthening, were almost impossible for my exhausted leg and my leg had to rely on those long contractions to step down a slope. There weren't any spasms in it, just a complete lack of power.

I gritted my teeth and tried to fight through the pain running through my left leg and the left side of my back. It would have probably been full-body pain, but I didn't have the receptors to feel its mirror image on my right side. I was also psychologically exhausted from concentrating so hard for so many hours, and controlling my body weight on the way down was pushing me so much further towards my limit. After the fifth step, wincing in pain the whole time, my right leg gave way. I collapsed to the ground.

Nausea pushed at my stomach and I leant over and retched, but nothing came out. My body didn't have anything to give. I retched again. Nothing. Exhaustion held me down and my mind sluggishly tried to make sense of our situation.

We were hours from camp 2 and had only taken five steps. I had reached my limit and my leg could no longer hold me up. When I was a rugby player, I had always taken pride in pushing myself during pre-season training. I would be at the gym every day, doing relentless squats and the most savage leg sessions you could imagine. Often, I'd hobble out of the gym, but I'd never had one of my legs go from under me. The reason I could push even further now was because of my lack of sensation on that side of my body. Normally, people stop because the build-up of lactic acid in their legs is causing them so much pain. Without that feedback signal, there was no warning from my leg. It went as far as it could take me and then simply refused to work anymore. And I couldn't use my arms to help it along, either. I needed them for my walking poles, which were essential to stop me from tumbling down the mountain.

I began to shake and felt an emotional flood reach my eyes. The intensity of it all threatened to overwhelm me. I was physically, psychologically and neurologically exhausted. But there were no tears; I was too dehydrated to produce them. I had hoped we had finished with the excruciatingly difficult bit and were into a new, slightly easier stage, but unfortunately that wasn't the case. The descent was going to be just as hard as the ascent – and there was a vast amount of 'descent' still to go.

'Are you alright, mate?' Arron asked.

I glanced up at him and Shyam, who had matching looks of concern.

'It might be hypothermia,' Shyam said. 'Big problems if it is because you could pass out.'

I shook my head. 'It's not hypothermia. My nervous system is fried.'

It took a bit to convince them, but I was certain it wasn't hypothermia. No one knew my body as well as I did. I could see how worried Arron and Shyam were and how much my inability to get down the mountain would impact and possibly endanger them. A protective mode kicked in. We had just under five hours of daylight left and I realized we would be travelling well into the night. We needed to get moving or it could become even more hazardous. Because my stronger leg had decided to bow out, I couldn't even hop down – my left leg couldn't sustain that pressure.

'Could I slide?' I asked.

The slope's gradient was about forty degrees, so there was no way I could free slide because if I got up enough speed, I wouldn't be able to stop. Secondly, there were crevasses to deal with. The only way was to stay roped up and be lowered down.

Shyam was already attached to the fixed line and quickly slipped the rope's end through my harness. I would then be free of the fixed line but also have the security of being attached to it via Shyam. It was the sort of setup a guide might use if someone had a fractured leg, which my right leg was doing an excellent job of mimicking. All of this would mean I could slide sitting down without building up so much momentum that I would skid right off the mountain. This was clearly not a tobogganing situation.

I faced the descent and gingerly pushed myself off. Small slides were best, closer to a shuffle. Still, we made good progress for half an hour until we reached the first crevasse slicing its way across our path.

I slowly got to my feet and stared into the slither of darkness below. Unlike on the way up, I wasn't concerned about whether I could step over it as I knew that gravity would help with that. It was stopping that was going to be a problem.

'Just give me some slack,' I said to Shyam. 'I'm going to go for it, but my legs won't support my weight with that sort of momentum. Once I'm over, I'll fall and begin to slide, so you'll have to stop me with the rope.'

He nodded and braced himself, digging his crampons into the ice.

I lurched forward with all the strength my right leg had left and touched down on the far side. Immediately, my leg gave way beneath me and I tipped forward. I tried to protect my neck and landed on my stomach. The force of the fall pushed me forward and I began to slide – fast. At any moment, I expected to feel the tug of the rope, but there was nothing. I kept on sliding, head first, picking up pace. Had Shyam let go of the rope? Was this it?

No matter how exhausted you are, it's amazing how quickly your brain wakes up when the scent of death is in the air. I tried to turn myself around so my feet were facing down the mountain so that I could dig my ice axe into the ground. I knew if I turned around, the last thing I should do was dig my crampons in, which could have flipped me into the air and right over. But as I reached around, I felt the sudden yank of the rope and I snapped to a stop.

To be fair to Shyam, I hadn't specified how much slack I wanted. With my heart still racing, I sat and waited for them to catch up. Once they had, I dragged myself to my feet and tested my leg. It would only hold my weight for a few steps before buckling, so I resorted to sitting down and sliding along again, with Arron and Shyam following me. It was much quicker than walking, anyway.

The views surrounding us constantly enticed me to stop and admire them. Now that we were on our way down, we were no longer staring at our feet and a snow slope. Instead, we were facing panoramic vistas of Nepal rolling out in front of us for hundreds of miles. The contrast between the beauty surrounding us and the seriousness of our situation was mind-boggling. Like a siren song, I had to avoid getting caught up in it. All the mountain ranges in the distance were clearly visible and it felt like the whole world was beneath us. We just had to get there.

Fortunately, over the next three hours, there was only one further crevasse and I told Shyam to give me less rope. It was then back to testing my leg for a few steps before sliding on my bum. Pride didn't even come into it. I knew I needed to get down that mountain as quickly as possible and this was the most efficient way to do it.

We spoke only to give instructions to each other. We were all feeling the pressure and when we did stop to eat one of our few remaining snack bars, I had to scoop snow into my mouth with every bite as I was so dehydrated. Without that small amount of moisture, I couldn't chew or swallow. I had already poured the last drops of water into my mouth a while ago and my bottle was empty. We had required far more water than anticipated and nearly all of us had run out. We also didn't have a burner to melt the snow and shoving huge quantities of it into your mouth actually does more damage than good, as it drops your temperature. I knew it would be hours until I tasted liquid again.

None of us said it, but we all knew our situation was serious. There were no surprises about our route back. We were all aware of what was coming and how far we had to go to get back to camp 2: down the fixed ropes to the piece of flat ground where we saw the view of Tibet, across the flat and down the fixed line with the gradient that had nearly finished me off, past where camp 3 would have been, across the vast glacier filled with crevasses and along the broad ridge (also filled with crevasses). We were still at stage one on the first set of fixed ropes.

I must have shuffled and slid for about three hours until finally, at 5 p.m., we reached the shoulder where the slope flattened out. We all slumped to the ground. After a minute or so, I glanced behind me to see how far we had come. In the distance were two figures.

'It's Beetle and Bigraj,' I said. 'I thought they would have caught up with us by now.'

Arron turned to look behind him. 'I wonder how high they got?'

With a little over ninety minutes of daylight left, we didn't have time to find out. We needed to continue along the shoulder towards the last pitch with the fixed rope before the glacier. Without gravity to help slide me down the mountain, I would have to walk. I stood up and prayed the three hours of rest would have brought some life back into my right leg. If it hadn't, we were screwed.

Arron helped pull me up and I took a step. It was feeling

a bit better and I slid my left leg forward to meet my right one, my crampons catching on the snow despite them being filed down. We didn't have time to stop to admire Tibet again, but it took us a solid half hour to pass the view, so there was still an opportunity to appreciate its splendour.

In good time, we reached the first slope we had jumared up the night before. I peered down at it. In the waning daylight, I realized it was much steeper than I remembered and could understand why I had found it so difficult coming up.

Shyam went first, clipping into the fixed line and using his descender to make his way down. On the way up, the jumar we had used was an ascender and on the way down, we switched to a descender, where the teeth ran in the opposite direction. It was my turn next and I attached my descender to the line and turned around. When going down a steep fixed line, you approach it like a ladder and face the slope. I pulled the small lever on the descender and it released some of the rope running through it. Leaning back, I took my first backwards step – and fell to my knees.

I looked up at Arron. 'I don't know how I'm going to do this.'

Using a different set of muscles was too much for my legs, which had buckled beneath me. Shyam was already at the end of the fixed line and he had our one 150-foot length of rope with him, so there was no chance of lowering me.

'Could you slide again?' Arron said.

'No, it's too steep.' I thought for a moment. 'Perhaps I could slide on my front and use my ice axe to slow my descent.'

I showed Arron what I meant by turning onto my stomach and unclipping the ice axe from my harness. I then tucked it under my shoulder. The sharp, pointy end was facing downwards and the flat, rounded end used for digging out the snow was nestled in the crook of my shoulder. Most mountaineers use their ice axe while going uphill, but I rarely use it as I need both walking poles to steady myself. So far, I had primarily used mine to get me out of crevasses and it was now acting as a kind of shoulder crampon.

'That could work,' Arron said. 'Do you want to give it a go?'

'It's the only way I can think of.'

I unclipped myself from the fixed line, my safety net, and carefully pushed myself forward. I would never normally have unclipped from a fixed line, but the slope was only fifty metres and there was a large flat section below it that would halt my progress if I did lose control. I carefully pushed myself forward, testing how far I needed to bury the axe. The harder I pushed down, the slower I went and when I found myself picking up speed, I used my new brake.

It wasn't easy, but it worked and I soon found myself in a heap at the bottom of the slope. I lay back exhausted and stared at the clear blue sky, wondering how the hell my body was still going. Arron soon slumped down next to me, having chosen to descend the traditional way rather than the penguin-on-ice way.

'Here,' he said, offering me half of his last energy bar.

I packed in a mouthful of snow and took a bite. I chewed slowly, trying to imagine every last calorie entering my stomach and fuelling my body.

I had never reached that level of exhaustion before. All my body wanted to do was shut down and sleep. Just for ten minutes. No longer than that, it promised. To switch off for a few minutes and recharge would be so nice. It was a glimpse

of how easy it was to become a body on a high-altitude mountain, as those were probably the final thoughts of many people
who had exhausted themselves in one of the most inhospitable
environments on the planet. I'm sure most of them didn't plan
on not waking up. But altitude can muddle the minds of far
more skilled and experienced climbers than me, particularly if
they were alone without people around them to influence their
decisions. If you fell asleep in a situation like the one I was in,
there was a pretty good chance you wouldn't wake up. On
Everest alone, there are an estimated 200 to 300 bodies, some
still visible to other climbers. The rescue missions are incredibly
dangerous and expensive as it can take ten hours to release the
ice's hold on the body and then around eight climbers to get
the person down. There are a lot of traumatic ways to die on
a mountain if you fall or there is an avalanche, but many people
just sit down for a rest and drift away. It comforted me to know
that some of the souls would have slipped off peacefully into
the unknown. At the same time, it made me recognize how
precarious our situation was and how grateful I was not to be
by myself.

As if on cue, Shyam spoke.

'We need to keep moving. I will quickly check the route.
Then come back. Five minutes.'

I nodded – the effort to speak seeming too much. As the
first people on Himlung for over two years, the route curving
around the corner was less clear than it would have been later
in the season. It was particularly challenging as Shyam had only
done the route once before after fixing the lines.

'We're getting there,' Arron said, swallowing the last bite
of his energy bar.

I watched as Shyam picked his way around the curve of the mountain before I lay down again. It wouldn't be long until I had to stand up and I honestly didn't know if I could do it.

Shyam was only fifteen metres away when he let out a blood-curdling scream.

I sat up and stared at Arron. 'He's not roped up to us.'

CHAPTER 15

Dusk

I knew straight away that Shyam must have fallen down a crevasse. There was no other explanation for his muffled scream growing fainter. Neither Arron nor I wanted to voice the question of how far he had fallen.

'Shyam!' Arron shouted, standing up.

We listened for a response, but there was nothing.

'Shyam! Are you okay?' Arron called again. He turned to me. 'I don't know which crevasse he went down.'

'Help!' came a faint response.

'Oh, thank God,' Arron said. 'He's alive.'

There was more shouting but we couldn't make out what Shyam was saying. My head was swirling. I knew how extreme the situation was, but I didn't think I could even stand to help.

'He must be deep,' Arron said, staring at the route Shyam had taken. 'I can't even hear what he's telling us to do.'

'Hold on!' I shouted as loudly as I could. 'Are you hurt?'

I looked at Arron and then at the rope on the floor between us. I could hardly hold myself up, never mind pull someone out of a crevasse. If Arron went over he might fall too, but we couldn't just leave Shyam there.

'Where's Bigraj and Beetle? I said.

We both turned around to look back up the slope and, right on cue, they appeared on the ridge above us.

'Shyam's fallen down a crevasse!' we both shouted at the same time.

Their smiles dropped. You could tell that wasn't the news they were expecting. With all the reserves they could muster, they made it down the fixed line as quickly as they could.

Beetle was as white as a sheet and didn't look well.

'You okay?' I asked.

He stared at me blankly and nodded slowly.

Bigraj was already gathering up the rope for us to tie in together. There were crevasses all around, but we had to get over to Shyam. To do that, we had to protect each other by being roped up. I gritted my teeth, pushed myself up, and Bigraj clipped me and the others to the rope.

He led the way, shouting reassuringly to Shyam in Nepali. We slowly made our way towards the hole in the snow, guided by Shyam's voice.

I felt the yank on my harness before I saw what happened. I had been so focused on my feet and trying not to collapse, I hadn't seen anyone else fall through the snow. I lurched back-wards against the pull on my harness and sat against the slope.

Arron was up to his waist in snow ten metres ahead of me, dangling over the edge of a dark crevasse.

'I don't know if I can hold myself for much longer!' he shouted, while scrabbling to pull himself out.

Half delirious, I shuffled backwards to put more tension on the rope while Bigraj turned around to do the same on the other side. We watched as Arron clawed at the snow with his gloved hands, his legs trying to find some purchase – a ledge, anything

– to help him clamber out. All the while Shyam was still calling for Bigraj, probably wondering why we hadn't reached him yet. The snow was dropping away from either side of Arron and it looked as though he was sinking. How was I going to pull him out when I couldn't even hold my own body weight?

Arron stared up at me with a genuine look of fear. He took a few deep breaths to calm himself and then started to make small, intentional movements. We leant back on the rope from both sides and with a considerable amount of shuffling, dragging and pulling, Arron did the job and was free to crawl back to the only stretch of ground we were confident was safe.

We were completely surrounded by unanticipated crevasses. The night before, we had been able to walk over them thanks to the freezing temperatures, but now they'd had a day's worth of sun, the surface was a minefield of hidden holes. I didn't know how we would get out of there when it felt like dusk was chasing us.

'I will get to Shyam,' Bigraj said to us. 'I think I know which crevasse it is.'

Thankfully, Bigraj was only a few metres from our lost climbing guide. We all watched, wondering if we would see Bigraj suddenly drop as well. He took the last ten steps while we all held our breath. Finally, he reached Shyam and bent to peer down a small slit less than two feet in width.

Bigraj spoke quickly with Shyam in Nepali before throwing down the end of the rope for him to attach to his harness.

'What can you see?' Arron shouted to Beetle, who was the closest to Bigraj.

'It's pitch black apart from Shyam's head torch at the bottom,' Beetle shouted.

He was still keeping his distance so if Bigraj fell down the crevasse, Beetle could break his fall and not get pulled in with him.

Bigraj filled in the details. 'Shyam is moving around. I think he is okay. His ice axe is sticking out from one of the walls of the crevasse. His other one is further down on the other wall.'

My stomach rolled at the thought of the ice axes in the crevasse walls. I couldn't imagine Shyam's terror when his hand slipped from the second axe. He wouldn't have known how far he would fall. Another metre or a hundred?

'Is he hurt?' Arron shouted.

Bigraj stood to secure the other end of the rope he had thrown down the hole. 'He tells me he is okay physically. He didn't break his legs because the crevasse is narrow. It stopped him from falling fast. He also managed to slow himself in two places.' He nodded to Shyam's ice axes. 'But we have a big problem. He is ten metres down.'

'Is he on a ledge?' Arron asked.

'No. He got lucky. The crevasse is only ten metres deep, so he is on solid ground.'

It turned out Shyam had been incredibly lucky. If he had fallen unroped in the middle of the glacier, he would probably have already been dead. But because we were right on the edge of it, the ice was only ten metres deep as the bedrock is much higher on the side of the valley. That was probably the reason he hadn't roped up to us in the first place. He had thought it was safe on the slope as there were far fewer crevasses at the edge of the glacier before it flattened and the tension that caused the fractured ice began.

Bigraj began heaving on the rope to help pull Shyam out.

I could feel the adrenaline seeping out of my body and was struggling to stay awake. I glanced over to Beetle and Arron, who were sitting down nearby and leaning back on the ropes in case Bigraj fell down the crevasse. They were both hunched in on themselves and I imagined they too were exhausted. Inside the crevasse, I could hear Shyam digging in his crampons and trying to help himself up the crevasse wall. It was also lucky that he was a professional mountaineer. If any of us had fallen, we might not have had the skills to climb out.

'He has reached his ice axes!' Bigraj called after thirty minutes.

From then on, Shyam made swift work of climbing the crevasse wall and it was a huge relief when his head poked up above the surface of the ice. He was shaken but he still managed to force a smile. We all gathered on the stretch of ice we knew to be safe and Shyam told us he only had a few bumps and bruises. He was clearly exhausted after all the strain of climbing out of the crevasse on top of the day we'd had. He was also the guide who had been up to fix the lines, so he had pretty much climbed Himlung twice.

'We take a ten-minute break,' Bigraj announced before sitting next to Shyam and speaking to him quickly in Nepali.

As I watched them talk, I began to imagine what would have happened if Shyam had broken a leg or an arm. He wouldn't have been able to help climb out and it would have fallen on Bigraj to pull him out of the deep crevasse. I didn't even know if that would have been possible. The alternative scenario woke me up a bit and I leant over to Beetle.

'Are you okay?' I asked. An adrenaline surge spiked through me and I felt the overwhelming need to check that everyone was alright. 'You looked as white as a ghost when I first saw you coming down the mountain.'

My words took a while to register and Beetle turned slowly to me. 'Just knackered, mate. That's all.'

'How far up did you get?' I asked.

'I didn't manage to get to the summit,' he said quietly. 'We stopped at the end of the fixed line, about two hundred metres from the top. It was too dangerous to keep going without having something to clip onto and Bigraj didn't have any rope to continue fixing the line.'

It was completely understandable that they hadn't gone any further. If there had been fixed lines all the way to the top, Beetle would have stood a chance as he was dealing well with the altitude and was incredibly fit. A much more experienced mountaineer might have used their ice axes and continued that way. I thought about what we would have done if we had all got to the end of the fixed line. Perhaps if the snow conditions had been much better, Shyam would have told us to rope up to each other and continue that way.

'Bigraj is exhausted,' Beetle said. 'He was taking oxygen on the way up. The guides have to do so much more than us and I think it's taking its toll.'

I lay back on the ground, appreciating my thick down trousers and jacket. There was hardly any wind and I was actually quite warm. The adrenaline was wearing off again and I didn't know what was coming next. Realising the danger in that line of thinking, I turned my thoughts to how we often assumed that people who were born in Nepal were so used to the altitude and physical exertion that they didn't ever feel fatigue. Quite often, I'd hear people refer to any Nepalese person who goes up a mountain as a 'Sherpa', but that isn't the case. Sherpas are an ethnic group who live up on the border with Tibet. Traditionally, they were the people the original Western mountaineers hired to accompany them, but somehow the word has become misused by many to describe any Nepalese porter or mountain guide. None of the guides or porters with us were Sherpas, they were just incredibly skilled Nepalese climbers. But, just like any human, they got tired too and they had been climbing much more than us with far heavier loads. I glanced over at Shyam and Bigraj and wondered what they were thinking. How tired were they? Would they even tell us?

'I want to apologize,' Beetle said out of the blue.

'What for?' I couldn't think of anything he needed to apologize for.

'I shouldn't have continued up the mountain. I should have stayed with you. I'm here as a professional cameraman and I should have stayed with you. That's what the filming is about. Not getting me to the top.'

I tried to smile but then realized my buff was covering my mouth.

'Don't be silly,' I said. 'It's fine. You'd come so far and it was right to see if you could summit.'

I couldn't say any more as my body suddenly felt like lead. Dusk was on the horizon and as I struggled to sit up, I wondered how I would ever be able to stand. I gave up and sank back into the snow. Arron and Beetle shuffled closer to me and the three of us sat together as we waited to be told what to do next. We were in our guides' hands.

Arron called Bigraj over. 'I'm worried about Ed,' he said. 'I don't think he can walk any further. His body is so tired that if he falls into a crevasse, he's not going to be able to help get himself out.'

I was too depleted to interrupt or add my viewpoint and just quietly listened. Perhaps Arron was right.

'If we carry on,' Arron said, 'and Ed falls in a crevasse, which is likely as we're completely surrounded by them, it's going to be really hard for us to pull him out. He weighs a lot more than Shyam.' Beetle nodded. 'If any of us fall down a crevasse it will put a lot of risk on the rest of the team.'

'I have been thinking the same thing,' Bigraj said looking over at Beetle. 'All of you struggling. I think we might need to call a helicopter. I'll speak to Shyam, but I agree that we can't go any further at the moment.'

Hearing Arron and Bigraj talk about me while I was there made me realize I was in a worse state than the rest of them. It meant they were now in charge of my safety. I buried my chin deeper into my jacket as I tried to process what this meant.

The gravity of our situation hit me.

We didn't have any water, shelter or food. We hadn't slept for thirty-six hours and our bodies were battered and bruised from days of gruelling climbs. We only had one of our mountain guides with us and it was just the five of us left. No one could have predicted this set of circumstances and they couldn't have been prevented. Some days the mountains just won't let you pass. I knew what we were facing up there could easily take us as close to death as I had been in that ambulance after my accident.

The natural adrenaline racing around my body after everything that had happened in the past few hours was wearing off.

I began to shake uncontrollably. Full body judders that were impossible to hide. I pulled deep into myself, becoming less aware of my surroundings and more focused on my breathing and racing heartbeat. It was a mental game now, one where I had to stop my mind from tipping me over into terror. One of my friends helped me to sit, while the other leant away from us and vomited. It was tinged with blood. I hoped that if it was altitude sickness, it didn't develop into high-altitude pulmonary edema, which was life-threatening.

I couldn't control my body as it continued to shake. Even with my fogged mind, I knew I was going into shock. I peered at my friends through the small slit left for my eyes between the insulated hat pulled down over my eyebrows and the seamless material of the buff that covered my mouth all the way up to the bridge of my nose. We were all clearly exhausted. Someone handed me an oxygen mask, but my body wouldn't respond to the simple signal I sent to reach out to it. I couldn't move my arms to take the mask, just like when I was paralyzed at the bottom of the pool and couldn't push myself to the surface.

A few metres away, I heard the beeps of the satnav phone.

Bigraj spoke into it in Nepali, moving further away from us to try and get a clear signal.

Relief flooded through me that the decision had been made to call in a helicopter and help was on its way. In all my years of climbing, I have never needed to have a helicopter sent out, but I knew there wasn't any other option. Someone pulled the mask onto my face as my body continued to judder. I imagined the oxygen flooding my veins and filling my muscles, travelling around the corners of my body that had been starved of it for so long. The beep of the satnav phone and muffled conversation reassured me that we were not alone.

I could feel myself wanting to sleep again even though it wasn't yet twilight, just as I had in the back of the ambulance five years ago. I could see it in my friends' hunched forms. We were all struggling to stay awake, but we knew falling asleep without a tent was how you died at these altitudes. Your core temperature dropped when you slept and that was something we couldn't risk getting any lower when we would soon be subjected to temperatures of around -25°C. We would have to burrow into ourselves, drawing on our last reserves for another hour or two while we waited for the helicopter to arrive.

Bigraj picked his way over to us in the knee-high snow and began to speak. I followed his lips but couldn't trace the words.

Dazed, I pulled the mask from my face, relieved my arms were working again. 'Say it again.'

'We must wait until morning,' he repeated. 'The sun will set any minute. The helicopters cannot fly at night because the mountains are too high here. They say they cannot make it before it gets dark.'

'Is there nothing we can do to make them change their minds?'

Before he answered, I already knew it was pointless. They would have come if they could.

'No, nothing can change their minds. Even when they set off in the morning, the highest most helicopters can fly is 6,000 metres. So, it is good we have already come down this far. In the morning, I will try to find a safe landing spot for them.'

Questions circled my mind. Would the snow freeze overnight to cover the crevasses and enable us to cross them? Was the pilot experienced in landing so high? Would the helicopter be stripped back so it was light enough to reach us?

I rolled onto my side and stared at the heavy orange sun beginning to set just above the mountains. Sunset and sunrise happened more quickly here as we were closer to the equator. Once the sun travelled below the mountains, we would be plunged into -25°C for twelve hours. My hands and feet had been numb for hours and I imagined it creeping up my arms and legs, meeting in the middle.

I hadn't given up. None of us had, but the responsibility for my friends' safety weighed heavily on me. No one else had been in danger when I dived into that pool and there was no risk of taking anyone else with me. But it was not just me who had to get through the night. My friends did as well and the chances of survival were slim. To try and keep myself and the others awake, I began to hum one of the songs that had helped me through the long weeks in a hospital bed.

The sun slipped below the horizon, leaving us to the night.

CHAPTER 16

The Night

As I hummed Bob Marley's 'Three Little Birds', the initial shock of our situation passed and a calm acceptance washed over me. After all the uncertainty and confusion, we now had a singular focus – to survive until morning.

I wanted to see another day; I wanted to rise up for another morning. But I also knew it wasn't guaranteed. Slowly sitting up, I looked over to Arron, then Beetle who had a patch of orange snow near him where he had thrown up. Neither of them was visibly panicked despite understanding the severity of the situation. Perhaps all of us knew there was no point in freaking out. We'd just burn through more calories and potentially endanger ourselves further. Or perhaps we were all too exhausted to feel any outrage or fear. All I knew was that it would be a mighty shame if we didn't get to see the sun rise again.

Bigraj and Shyam were sitting slightly further away, huddled together and talking rapidly in Nepali. I didn't know what they were saying, but it sounded like they were exploring some options.

I was about to ask Beetle how he was feeling when I began to shake again, my nervous system juddering back into life. Arron and Beetle shuffled closer to me so they could share their body warmth. We were like three penguins packed together on the ice, not a millimetre of space between us. There were no thoughts of 'This is it', but as I sat there uncontrollably shaking, I knew that given our circumstances and the state we were in, it would be almost impossible for us all to stay awake for another night. The simple fact was, if we fell asleep, it was likely we would die as our core temperature would drop so low our hearts would stop beating. But there was still the word 'almost' there. It wouldn't be impossible to stay awake for another night; it would be *almost* impossible, which meant there was still a chance. Having had a keen interest in adventure and exploration since my accident, I had heard enough survival stories to know that people had pulled themselves through much worse. This gave me hope despite there being no denying we were in a precarious position, especially for three very wet-behind-the-ears novices. Two years before, when Himlung was last climbed, an incredibly experienced Spanish mountaineering guide died on the descent from exhaustion and hypothermia.

It was Arron who spoke first. 'I'll go through our supplies.'

He took each of our backpacks from us and meticulously went through everything we were carrying. Once he had finished, he made us each sit on a backpack to try to insulate us further from the ice.

Neatly laid before us was the sum total of what we had left: 200ml of water, a small bag of gummy sweets and one energy bar.

'It's better than nothing,' he said, before tucking everything into his summit suit to ensure it didn't freeze. 'We just need to get through to sunrise and then the helicopter can land.'

Beetle nodded. I tried to nod, but I was shaking so much it was difficult to make it stand out from all of the judders my body was going through. The constant movement was exhausting and I could feel the cold seeping in. What we really needed was some shelter. The air was perfectly still, but I knew we would be in grave danger if the wind picked up. There wasn't any loose snow nearby for us to dig out a snow hole, which had saved the life of many a mountaineer before us. If we had been lower down, we might have been able to do it, but that would mean getting to the glacier, which brought obvious dangers. Digging into ice would have expended more energy than it was worth while the air was so still. I decided to raise it as a possibility if the weather turned, as the risk versus reward ratio would change.

Beetle was leaning on my shoulder. He looked unwell and even paler than usual. I gave him a couple of nudges in case he had fallen asleep. I couldn't form words, but a nudge was enough and he shifted slightly, letting me know he was still with us.

I began to cough uncontrollably, my body throwing a new symptom of altitude into the mix.

Bigraj and Shyam both stood and picked their way over to us.

'We are going to camp 2,' Bigraj said. 'We get more water, food, blankets and a tent and then come back. I managed to radio Kaji but could not get through to base camp.'

'Are you sure you should go?' Arron said. 'Is it safe for you?'

'We will rope up together,' Bigraj said confidently. 'We will be fine. Be back in four to five hours.'

'Thank you,' Arron said. 'And be safe.'

'Here,' Bigraj said, pulling an oxygen mask over my face and leaving it there. 'You have this for a while. It keep you warm and maybe help with the cough.'

I didn't know if he had another one for himself, but I hoped he did. As I sat breathing the oxygen in, a boost of clarity and warmth crept around my body. My cough receded enough for me to slow my breathing. I thought about how the additional oxygen might have helped me get to the top of Himlung. With my neurological difficulties, I didn't know why I was so worried about levelling the playing field with people who had fully functioning legs, arms and hands. But I knew I had made the right decision on the way up. Once descending the mountain, I didn't see any point in self-righteously staying away from oxygen – it was now a matter of survival.

With the mask strapped over my face, I watched as our guides slipped the rope through their harnesses, buried their chins into their jackets and set off into the distance until only their head torches were visible. In my mind, I traced their route past camp 3, where the Spanish guide from two years ago had sadly passed away, then across that vast glacier and along the broad ridge – both filled with crevasses. I sent up a small prayer that they would be okay and that the mission they had set themselves would be worth it.

In what seemed to take a huge amount of effort, I pulled back the edge of my jacket sleeve to check the time. It had just gone 8 p.m. Ten hours until sunrise. That small effort having exhausted me, I wanted to close my eyes but knew I couldn't. It was too tempting – I would fall asleep straight away. I just had to stay awake until the sun could warm us and there was a hugely reduced risk from sleeping.

There was a time shortly after my accident, when I couldn't move anything below my neck, when I thought it would have been better if I had died that day at the bottom of the pool. I had never voiced it as I knew it would be too painful for my family to know at the time. I might have made a joke around it, but I could never say that underneath the humour lay a bedrock of truth. I thought it would be better if I could have been pulled out of existence rather than being a burden to my mum and Lois for the rest of my life. I didn't realize that all they desperately wanted was for me to live, to stay with them. On the mountain, it was entirely different. I didn't want to leave. I had built a life worth living for, fighting for, and if you had shown that young man in the hospital bed what was possible, he would have fought for it too. Perhaps he did.

I could feel Arron draping some spare jumpers over me as I shook. I was sure it was my nervous system, but perhaps it was hypothermia. I didn't know anymore. All I knew was that it was exhausting not being able to remain still. I sucked in the oxygen and hoped it would settle the misaligned signals firing around my body.

Beetle turned and threw up rust-coloured liquid in the snow. Mucus mixed with blood.

I pulled my oxygen mask off.

'How long...throwing up blood?' I said slowly.

Beetle wiped his mouth. 'That was the third time. Once earlier with you.' He paused to catch his breath. 'First time coming down the mountain with Bigraj.'

'It's good we're lower. It will help.'

Of course, Beetle would know why I said that. What I didn't want to say was that we weren't low enough. We had all been suffering from mild effects of altitude, such as headaches, difficulty sleeping, a loss of appetite, tiredness and dizziness. That was part of being up high. When Ben had thrown up, Shyam and Bigraj had made the call that he couldn't go any further. Beetle throwing up mucus with blood in it meant he could be on the cusp of high-altitude pulmonary edema or already suffering from it. Our guides had spoken to us about this earlier and told us what to look out for. This potentially fatal illness is caused by ascending too fast. The capillaries in the lungs begin to leak, filling them with blood until you can't breathe anymore – a horrible way to go.

'Let's swap places,' Arron said to Beetle.

Without questioning it, Beetle shuffled around to my right side and Arron was now on my left. I was clearly going to remain the middle part of this penguin sandwich. Knowing that made me realize Arron was worried about me, or we would have taken turns in the middle where there was body heat from both sides. Arron had moved Beetle away from the more exposed side and taken that one himself. He was undoubtedly in the best state of all of us, but I don't think Beetle and I would have recognized our positioning if he hadn't mentioned it.

I took the oxygen mask off and, with a shaky hand, passed it to Beetle, who took in a few deep pulls.

'That's a bit better,' he said afterwards. 'I'm sure I'll be fine. Doing those extra hours up the peak just knackered me out.'

I thought about what would have happened if I had continued going up Himlung and ignored that crystal-clear call to turn around. If I'd given in to stubbornness and continued, my right leg would have been even more reluctant to help me on the way down. I could have easily ended up in a crevasse, resulting in a rescue mission for the others. All our lives would have been in danger through the delay. I knew Bigraj would have put his own life at alarming levels of risk to get me out, just as he was possibly doing now to get us extra supplies.

'You can't sleep, mate,' Arron said to Beetle, who had closed his eyes. I gave Beetle a few nudges with my shoulder and he lifted his head.

'Here was me thinking we could just call a helicopter and it would arrive,' Arron said. 'I must have thought they could fly at night with infrared or something. I didn't realize how dangerous it was for the pilots, even in the day.

'It's not windy tonight, thank God. That makes it just a waiting game.'

We both knew it could turn at any moment, though. If a storm came in, with our exposed position, the wind chill would drop the temperature by another ten degrees.

I lifted my nose from the depths of my jacket and looked up at the sky. Not a cloud in sight. The moon was rising and lit up the snowy peaks surrounding us. Its light reflected off the snow and created a silver glow so we could see far into the glacier and beyond. It was closer to an eclipse's illumination than the night's dark blanket. The snow glistened with ice crystals as though coated in thousands of diamonds. Pleased that my eyes were beginning to focus again, I realized we were at the bottom of a slope on a small ledge that acted like a bench. Behind me was the end of the last fixed line we had come down.

The silence, once I tuned into it, was overwhelming. There wasn't a single movement that could be heard; no human or animal sounds or leaves blowing in a breeze. Just pure, crystalized quiet. It was entirely peaceful and I thought that if the worst happened and I slipped away, it would certainly be a beautiful night on which to do it.

Arron nudged me before handing over a morsel of a snack bar and a sip of water. I had lost track of time and didn't want to focus on what was being held out in front of me. I imagined the icy liquid and sickly sugar in my mouth and grimaced. The stimulus to want to eat and drink had wholly switched off in the hours we had gone without both.

Arron continued holding it in front of me until I relented and took my sip before passing the water bottle to Beetle and placing the food in my mouth. The water was so cold it felt like it was burning me and immediately seemed to dissolve in my dry mouth. I didn't even seem to swallow it. The energy bar just sat on my tongue – a foreign object that did not belong there. It occurred to me how odd it was that we put objects inside of us and chewed on them. A bizarre way to go about it. Arron frowned and I reluctantly packed in some snow and began the laborious task of grinding down the sickly lump so I could eventually swallow it. Uck. I did not want to have to do that again. My eyes glazed over and I could feel myself being pulled towards sleep.

'Right,' Arron said loudly. 'Let's do some breathwork and seated qigong movements to help get us warm.'

We dutifully followed Arron's instructions. It was a good job we had been practising qigong over the weeks as the movements now came naturally with a bit of food and oxygen added into the mix. They did indeed bring back a small corner of focus in my mind. I checked my watch, just past 10.30 p.m.

'Have you thrown up again?' I asked Beetle.

'No,' he responded. 'But I'm starting to feel the cold seeping in.'

I felt it too. It was sinking deeper into me. My hands and

feet had been numb for hours despite the continuous shaking. I really hoped they weren't frostbitten. I did not want to 'lose toe' as Bigraj had so aptly put it. A crescendo of chattering teeth circled through us. It was as if once one of us acknowledged how cold it had become, our bodies suddenly caught up and began trying to warm us. Despite the constant chattering, every cell in my body wanted to sleep.

I nudged Arron with my left shoulder as he hadn't spoken for a while.

'Huh, what,' he said sleepily.

'Bigraj should be back soon,' I said. 'It's been a few hours.'

'Let's see who can spot his headlamp first,' Arron said.

'And the winner gets?' Beetle added.

To keep all their fingers and toes, I thought, but decided not to say it aloud. A sudden realization hit me and I groaned.

'What is it?' Arron asked, more alert.

'I've just realized that if we don't survive this, Lois is going to kill me!'

Beetle started laughing and then Arron joined in too.

'I think my mum will kill me,' Beetle added.

I laughed, but the realization of how many years we had on Beetle hit me. I was nearly ten years older than him and a lot had happened during those ten years. I suddenly, desperately, wanted Beetle to see them as well.

'Right,' I said to Beetle. 'You need to stay awake. I want you to tell me everything you know about cricket. And I know that is a lot. So, crack on.'

Beetle grinned, fully ready to educate us both. I already knew quite a lot about cricket as my childhood friend, Tom, had been cricket-mad. He was so good at it he'd even played it professionally. As Beetle slowly spoke, his sentences sometimes a little jumbled and taking the occasional pause, I enjoyed knowing that every word he uttered meant he was still there with us.

The cold set in and when Beetle ran out of words, I nudged him with my shoulder a few times.

My eyes closed and with a falling sensation, my brain shut off and I slumped forward.

Tom was sitting next to me. I hadn't seen him for years. Nine to be exact. I could have probably worked out the months and days, too, if the altitude wasn't messing with my head so much. I put my arm around him; there was no awkwardness between old friends. He grinned at me. I turned to my other side and Rich was there too – the three of us back together. I started tugging at my mitt so I could take off my jacket to show Tom the Russian-lettering tattoos Rich and I had got done for him after he died, but he stilled my hand. He already knew what we had done and that we were sorry we hadn't got the 'Brothers in Arms' tattoos when he first suggested them.

I blinked in the grey light and Tom morphed into Beetle, his hand on my glove, his eyes wide, trying to understand what I was doing.

It wasn't Tom.

Oh. But then, how could it be?

'Bloody hell,' I said quietly. 'I just fully hallucinated.'

'I thought you were going to take your glove off,' Beetle said.

'Thank God we're not on our own.'

I knew the story of this night would have been a very different one if we had been alone.

'I think I can see a headlamp,' Arron said. 'Over there.'

He pointed, but I couldn't see anything.

'Just over there,' Arron said. 'Can't you see it?'

We each stared into the dark.

After ten minutes, Arron said quietly, 'I must have been mistaken.'

It seemed I wasn't the only one who had started to hallucinate, which was another sign of altitude sickness. I hoped Bigraj was okay, wherever he was.

'Guys, guys!' Beetle said excitedly, nudging me so sharply my head rolled away from him and snapped back. 'Something amazing has happened.'

'What?' I said. 'Has Bigraj got back? Is he okay?'

'No,' Beetle continued. 'Look over there.'

I stared at the peak he was pointing to across from us.

'What?' Arron said.

'It's only the bloody Starship Enterprise. Landed over there. Ready to get us.'

Oh, fuck. Beetle had started hallucinating too. I checked my watch. Exactly midnight. How strange I had looked at it at the exact point a new day had ticked over.

'It's not real,' Arron said gently. 'Don't worry. I've just spent the last twenty minutes staring at a shadowy figure over there. I only realized it couldn't be real when there was no headlamp. Bigraj has a headlamp.'

I looked and nobody was on the glacier where he was pointing.

'The Enterprise had gone,' Beetle said dejectedly.

'Probably for the best, mate,' I said. 'Don't worry, the helicopter will be here soon. Much easier to land over this side.'

'Okay, guys,' Arron said. 'I definitely think it's Bigraj and not a hallucination. I've sense-checked it about a hundred times. The lamp is bobbing up and down and I'm sure it's getting closer.'

I lifted my head and stared over. 'I can see it! Beetle we need you in on this too.'

He briefly lifted his head. 'Definitely a headlamp.'

My spirits soared that our friend was okay. I stopped myself. Someone was okay. We didn't know it was Bigraj yet. We all watched carefully as they made their way to us, carefully picking their way through the snow. I almost held my breath as I knew that if they dropped into a crevasse, we would not be able to help them.

When they were ten metres away, I recognized who it was by their jacket in the silvery moonlight.

'Bigraj!' I shouted.

He took his last steps towards us and then slumped to the ground.

'Give him this,' I said to Beetle, as I passed the oxygen over.

Bigraj took a few breaths and we let him rest for a moment.

He pulled the mask away. 'Hello, my friends. Are you all okay?'

'We are,' Arron said. 'Are you okay?'

'Yes,' Bigraj said slowly. 'Very good luck on the way down. Before we got to camp 2, we met Kaji and the other expedition coming up for their summit push. They gave me some food and water. I sent Shyam and Kaji back to camp 2 to get a tent for you.'

I couldn't even imagine how Bigraj had made it halfway to camp 2 and back again when we three were struggling to sit up. I checked my watch. It was nearly 2 a.m. and he had been gone for almost six hours.

'Is Ben okay?' I asked.

'Yes, he is back at base camp. After Kaji dropped him off, he returned to bring us a little food and juice.'

'Here,' he said after digging it out of his bag.

There wasn't a lot, but enough for us to split it all fairly into four. As we slowly ate our small snack bars and drank the juice he had given us, Bigraj explained that he had been so worried about us that he didn't feel he could go on to camp 2 as he wanted to check we were all okay. Kaji had been roped up to the other expedition, so he wasn't by himself crossing the crevasse field. When Bigraj and Shyam had met Kaji on their way down, the two mountain guides had roped up to each other so they could go back down together and get a tent. Bigraj thought we wouldn't survive the night with our low energy levels, so that was why he had taken the huge risk of coming back by himself, unroped and across all those crevasses.

He huddled next to us, beside Beetle, so we could share our warmth with him. Despite us having just drunk more than we had in hours, no one had needed to pee for about twelve hours as our bodies were just absorbing all of the liquid that came to them. No one moved from our line of four and all we could hear were our clothes rustling as we nudged each other, trying to stay awake.

The temperature had significantly dropped. It wasn't the wind, as there was none. Instead, it was the icy cold seeping up through our bones from not moving. Despite the food, we were all still shivering even though we were practically sitting on top of each other. It wasn't a bad sign, though, as I knew we were all still okay if we were still moving. I'd once been told it was when you stopped shivering you should be worried, as your body was focusing solely on keeping your organs warm, which is the stage before dying.

In my exhausted mind, I decided I was done with the cold. It was time to take myself somewhere warm.

Lunch in Ibiza Town. The sun was shining and I was sitting in front of a plate filled with a whole cooked sea bass – it didn't get much better than that. I eyed my food and tucked a napkin into my T-shirt. A little sprinkling of rock salt and I was ready. Lois raised an eyebrow at me and smiled. She had seen this ritual a few times at this restaurant and knew I would work my way through most of what was in front of me. God, I was hungry. I grabbed a glass of water – thirsty, too. We had met the couple with us through our charity and they were now close enough friends to excuse me from making conversation for half an hour while I ate. It was a meal that deserved to be savoured. They chatted with Lois while I quietly worked through everything on my plate.

Leaning back, I patted my belly and looked around the table with a smile. 'To the beach!'

I lay down on the white sandy beach and popped my sunglasses on. A stripy towel beneath me and the girl of my dreams by my side. I had visited this fishing village in Croatia many times with my mum and was excited about taking Lois there. We'd only been dating for half a year, but she was fitting right in. My brother, Josh, and my mum, who we were travelling with, had accepted her with open arms and I could see Lois being 'the one'. I turned towards her. She was wearing a yellow bikini and when she saw me staring at her, she closed her eyes and smiled. I watched as she began to drift off to sleep.

Picking up a handful of sand, I thought about giving her a mermaid tail while she slept. No, too immature. Not something twenty-one-year-olds should do to their girlfriends. I released the sand and watched it pour between my fingers like an hourglass, mesmerized as if I could count every grain.

I picked up another handful of sand and watched it run from my hands.

'What are you doing?' Josh asked.

I stared up at him. He was young, nine or ten, perhaps. He was where Lois had been and, looking down at my body, I realized I was on the cusp of becoming a teenager.

'Shall I give you a mermaid tail?' I said.

He squealed and pelted into the sea, me following. I laid out flat and began the freestyle stroke that would get me ahead of him the quickest. We would swim out to the coral reef that had fascinated us the entire time we had been on holiday in Egypt with our mum and dad. Then, we would dive down and explore its hidden beauty.

A wave pushed me back toward the shore.

On the beach were my mum and dad on our first holiday in Cornwall. Josh, a plump baby, was sitting up on the sand. I raced through the low waves back to the bucket and spade beside him. Picking up the blue spade, I began digging up the sand. Josh grinned as I patted it around my legs, covering them in the diamond-like sand sparkling in the sun. I did my top half too. Just a bit more of my head to do, then I'd be completely buried in it. That would make Josh laugh.

'Ed,' Dad said gently. 'No more, it's not safe.'

I looked up at him, not understanding.

'Ed, wake up,' Arron said. 'You've stopped shivering. It's not safe.'

Something felt different. He was right. I had stopped shivering.

It was peaceful and I wanted to stay that way.

'More qigong,' Arron said briskly.

I followed his movements, but my mind was somewhere else. Our holiday in Cornwall was my first ever memory. There wasn't another one before that. I shivered at what would have come next if I had continued rewinding time. The familiar juddering began again.

To try and stay awake, I looked up at the glistening stars. It was the perfect night, apart from the cold. Ice crystals had started forming on my jacket. I realized I had never felt cold like it before and if the wind picked up, we'd be in big trouble. I stared out over the crevasse, trying to see if I could spot the headlamps returning with the tent, but I couldn't even hallucinate them. I was so tired.

A sparkling crust had formed on the snow and I wondered whether it would now be firm enough to cross. A pointless thought. Even if it was safer, we were so low on energy that if something went wrong, we would have almost no chance of correcting it.

*

I had lost all track of time. The seconds, minutes and hours all blurred together into one shivering haze as we tiptoed around the well of sleep we couldn't fall into.

My head was slumped forwards but my eyes still opened when Arron began pulling at my shoulder.

'Look, the light is changing!'

I raised my head slowly and sure enough, my eyes met the deep blues on the horizon. I looked over at Beetle, whose head was resting on my shoulder, and gave him a little nudge.

'Mate, it's coming. We made morning.'

We knew we weren't in the clear yet, but there was a palpable feeling of relief. Morning meant daylight and daylight meant warmth. One by one, the peaks began to light up, glowing red and reminding me of the embers of a campfire we had sat next to only a few nights before. Soon, they turned to orange, which spread down the mountainside to the valley below.

In what seemed like a matter of moments but must have been an hour, the shadows finally receded and the sun rose. I watched as the sunlight raced up the valley towards us, chasing the shadows away. Up it flew and I knew once the full force of the Himalayan light hit us, we were safe for that day. We watched as it travelled up the glacier and then across to us. As the bright sunlight hit us, we slowly uncurled from our cocoon of bodies and slumped back against the slope. Within moments, Arron and Beetle had fallen asleep, safe in the knowledge that the sunlight had quickly raised the temperature by around twenty degrees and there wasn't the same risk of us slipping off. Bigraj, still seated and looking like a prayer statue, fell asleep, exhaustion finally having taken hold of him.

Instead of making me sleepy, the light energized me and I decided to keep watch over my friends, waiting for the tantalizing vision of a helicopter coming to rescue us. After a night of delirium, I felt grounded again.

Although I hadn't said it to the others, I was very aware we weren't entirely out of the woods.

I let my friends sleep and looked to the horizon. After weeks of not wanting to see signs of human life, I was now desperate for them.

CHAPTER 17

Dawn

As I sat in the dawn light, watching the sun rise up in the sky, I wondered whether there would be any lasting damage after putting our bodies through that night. Arron had told me that he might have some frostbite to his toe, and we both agreed we would check his feet once we were off the mountain. We all looked as if we had fallen asleep on a sun lounger, with our skin bright red, peeling and chapped from sunburn, but that would heal. I just hoped we hadn't done any irreversible internal damage. Beetle hadn't thrown up for hours, so I was quite certain his altitude sickness hadn't developed into high-altitude pulmonary edema, which had been my most pressing concern.

Staring out across the valley, I felt hopeful. Because Bigraj had called for our helicopter the evening before, I knew we would be one of the first on the list. We had been told it would be with us around 8 a.m., so there wasn't long to wait. I imagined spotting a speck in the distance and waking my friends up to tell them it was all alright, we were getting off the mountain that day and wouldn't have to stay another night. I gazed intently at the horizon for the next hour, but there was no helicopter.

The other three eventually woke up around 8 a.m.

'Any sign of it?' Arron asked sleepily.

'No,' I said. 'It's still early and it's got to come all the way from Kathmandu.'

'It's funny,' Arron said. 'During the night, it felt like I had a purpose, which was to keep us all awake. And now that has passed, I feel zapped. I think this bit will be harder. I just want the helicopter to arrive so I don't need to worry about it anymore.'

'Have a sleep again if you want to, mate. We're okay now.'

He laid back and closed his eyes for another ten minutes.

Bigraj soon dragged himself to his feet and picked up a walking pole and ice axe.

The slope we were on was too steep to land a helicopter on and we knew there were at least two crevasses in front of us. The last thing we wanted was for the helicopter to land and crash through the snow. About thirty metres beyond the hole Arron had made when he fell through the snow was a gentle rolling mound that looked like it could be a crevasse-free option for a landing area.

'I will find a safe landing space,' Bigraj said.

'Be careful, mate,' Arron said, sitting up as Bigraj roped himself to us.

We watched as he tentatively approached the mound using the walking pole to test the snow before every step. Ten minutes later, he managed to circumnavigate the crevasse Arron had fallen into and was probing the area we thought could work. He had taken a different pole from his bag, one designed to find people in avalanches, but he had turned it into a crevasse probe. It unfolded to be a few metres in length and he was pushing it deep into the snow to see if there were any cavities below. Even though he was roped up, I could tell we were all anxious as we quietly watched him work; we were worried he would drop at any moment and I wasn't sure any of us had the strength to pull him out.

Around eighty metres away, he found a suitable spot for the helicopter and marked it out with the bags we had been sitting on.

He made his way back. He had taken a second incredible risk for us and we were all so relieved he was safe.

'Do you think Kaji and Shyam are okay?' Beetle asked.

Our two mountain guides had never returned.

'I think so,' Bigraj replied. 'When they coming back up, it may have been too risky for them, so they may have gone back to camp 2. I cannot contact them as my radio died last night. We will know once we get down.'

We sat in a line again and stared out at the horizon.

After half an hour, it was me who broke the silence.

'Do we need to call the helicopter again? Do they know they still have to come to us?'

'We are on their list,' Bigraj said. 'I gave them our GPS coordinates last night, so they will be able to find roughly where we are. But when we see the helicopter, we must jump up and wave.'

That all made sense. The helicopter didn't just have to make it to Himlung, it had to find us as well. The coordinates would guide them to us, but from high up, we would look like pinpricks on a whiteboard from the air. It would also be nearing its maximum flying altitude, so it was a risky job – one I hoped someone would be willing to take on.

By 9 a.m., we were all feeling unsettled. I had presumed that at first light, it would just set off and come straight to us, but it had been three hours since the sun had risen.

By 10 a.m., I had begun imagining what another night on the mountain would be like. I didn't know whether I could face it. Should I ask Bigraj if he could make it down to base camp and get help from there? I didn't know whether he had enough energy to get down safely. Would it help or endanger us?

I tried to push away the niggling worries and focused on quelling my anxiety. The helicopter had to come, because it was the only way I would make it off the mountain.

We heard it before we saw it. All this time, I had been staring into the distance, trying to spot the helicopter, and it was the sound that hit me first. The distant rumbling of it coming up the valley didn't feel real. We all glanced at each other for confirmation. It was 11 a.m. and the last fifty-two hours had been by far the greatest test of physical and psychological endurance I had ever faced. It was also the second time in my life I had stared my own mortality square in the eye.

A wave of euphoria rushed through me, but there was no time for contemplation or celebration as the most potentially dangerous part of our epic journey was about to unfold.

Helicopters suffer from altitude sickness too. They need oxygen to help with their lift and the reduced oxygen available high up makes them unstable. At 6,000 metres, we were towards the maximum height the standard models could fly to and with the additional danger of landing in a crevasse field, we would certainly be testing the pilot's skills. I was elated that one had decided to give it a go.

The sound of the rotors grew louder, but we still hadn't seen it yet. The deep whirring provided the boost of adrenaline we needed to drag ourselves to our feet. It was the first time I had stood in twelve hours and my legs were shaky, but at least my right leg had decided to start working again. Keeping our distance from each other, we slowly made our way over to Bigraj who had gone ahead to the landing site. Just as we got to him, we saw the helicopter for the first time that would take us to base camp, a tiny dot against a vast glacier rising from the valley below. How could something that far away already make so much noise? We grinned at each other; we hadn't all hallucinated its sound and it really was there to rescue us.

We all started waving with every last ounce of energy we could muster, praying he would spot us. The pilot tipped the nose of the red, white and blue chopper in our direction. Within moments, it was so close we could see the pilot looking left and right, scanning the ground for any sign of life. We'd had no contact with either base camp or mountain rescue since the previous evening due to the radio batteries dying in the cold, so the pilot wouldn't be sure whether it was a rescue or recovery mission. All thoughts of a recovery mission would have been dispelled when the pilot eventually caught sight of us. Arron had been flapping his arms so much it looked like he was about to take off and fly himself back to base camp.

The pilot flew straight over us before banking hard and circling back several times while assessing the situation. Eventually, he came close to the area Bigraj had marked with the bags about thirty metres in front of us. The updraft whipped icy snow all over us as the front skis of the helicopter touched the snow. The pilot then tentatively lowered the helicopter's full weight down. We held our breath, fully aware of how many crevasses could be around us and the consequences of finding one. I winced as the front of the chopper sunk hard into the snow and the landing skids disappeared beneath the surface.

But the pilot didn't seem fazed and when the cab met the snow, it came to a rest. He kept the motors whirring as he opened the door and signalled for two of us to go over.

Arron and I were first up. We hunched as low as we could and started making our way towards him. But my legs were still empty and walking in a crouch wasn't possible for me on a good day. As I got closer, I paused and looked up. The pilot was waving frantically. I caught his eye and he ran his thumb across his neck and pointed to the rotor.

Nothing quite like the international sign for 'you're about to die' to wake you up.

Tired and a bit delirious, we had failed to notice that due to the front of the helicopter sloping into the snow, the rotor blade was tilted forward about a metre from the floor and our necks were only a couple of metres away from it. Decapitation by chopper blade was not the end I had anticipated to our ordeal.

We both hit the deck and crawled the rest of the way.

Arron climbed in first and I dragged myself in behind him, shutting the cab door. Apart from the thin double seat we had slumped onto, the inside of the helicopter was stripped bare to make it as light as possible to fly at altitude. The pilot wasted no time in adding some torque to take off. The noise was deafening as the engine struggled to lift the front of the helicopter from the snow.

A few seconds later, he lowered the nose and turned to me in his yellow helmet.

'You, out.'

We were too heavy. He didn't know about my disability and I was the closest one to the door. In a situation like that, decisiveness can be the difference between life and death and the pilot knew exactly what he was doing. Without hesitating, I opened the door and flopped head-first into the snow.

I had only crawled a few metres away from the blades when the snow started to whip up around me again as the pilot pulled up hard. This time, the chopper was clear. I lifted my head from the snow and watched as the helicopter peeled back, banked and flew away, disappearing down into the valley as quickly as it had arrived.

Bigraj headed over and helped me to my feet.

I looked over to Beetle, who had his camera out and had been filming the whole thing.

'Well, that was exciting!' he said.

Before we knew it, the helicopter was back. This time, I crawled from the start, dragging myself through the door and slumping onto the seat. As we rose from the mountain, the scale of the land of giants revealed itself and Bigraj and Beetle became dots within a few seconds. I stared out of the window in shock as endorphins flooded through me. From the air, I could also see the shadows of the crevasses that were invisible from the ground. *What had just happened to us?* I traced our route from the defunct camp 3, to camp 2 to camp 1. Then, across the first glacier and the boulder fields that days before had nearly finished me off before we had even begun.

Soon afterwards, the yellow tents of base camp appeared. Below us, I could see people rushing out of them to the helicopter landing area. A third team was now at base camp and was helping on the ground, unsure of what state I would be turning up in. The helicopter set down. I squeezed the pilot on the shoulder, then shuffled to the door.

It was opened as soon as I reached it. Dil was standing there with his arm held out. I grabbed it and staggered forward as quickly as I could to clear the rotors. The pilot wasted no time taking off again. His job wasn't quite done. But for the first time, I felt an overwhelming sense of relief. I looked up to see Ben standing in front of me beside Arron, a massive grin on his face.

'Bloody hell, Ed. It's good to see you!'

It was good to see him, too.

It was Dil who first made the reality of what had nearly happened begin to sink in. He had tears in his eyes when he told us that after not hearing from us for almost two days, they had feared the worst. I looked around the crowd of porters, guides and climbers from the other expeditions. Beyond them, our base camp was crisscrossed in brightly coloured prayer flags, huge trails hanging between the tents. It was a real reminder that we had to respect the moment and the mountain. We were visitors and we were not there to conquer anything.

Dil noticed where my focus had gone. 'We put them up for you. We up all night praying.'

I was deeply touched by that level of compassion from people we had only known for a couple of weeks. We had all created such a strong bond they felt like family. The shock I felt was replaced by guilt as it registered what I must have put them through. My mind then moved to my family and Lois. Thank God they were still clueless about what had unfolded. The phone calls home, if we hadn't made it, didn't bear thinking about.

Before long, the helicopter was back and Bigraj and Beetle emerged. I was already on my third bottle of water and I handed them both one as they stumbled off the chopper. When I had landed, the craving for water still wasn't intense, but once I had started drinking, I realized how deep my thirst was. Something in my body had kicked back in and I couldn't get enough, to the point that I had to slow down as I was almost sick.

I felt a tension lift; we were all safe and, finally, we could begin to rest.

The pilot also needed a short break after the pretty hairy situation. It turned out he was an Austrian search and rescue and heli-ski pilot and after he had wrapped up the Austrian season, he switched to Nepal to do the opposite one. I hadn't realized that the vast majority of the rescue pilots in Nepal were European and I was grateful he had decided to use his skills to help us.

Soon, we were waving him off as we all traipsed into the kitchen tent where Kumar, our expedition cook, had been rustling up a special welcome-back lunch. Because we were all only exhausted and dehydrated, rather than injured or suffering from high-altitude pulmonary edema, none of us needed to go back with the pilot to Kathmandu hospital. All we needed was food, water and sleep, which were all available at base camp. Months ago, we had booked a helicopter large enough to take us all back to Kathmandu. We just needed to wait one more day for its arrival.

As we scoffed down the meal Kumar had carefully prepared for us, we all caught up on what had happened. There was a celebratory atmosphere. Kaji and Shyam told us about how they had managed to get down to camp 2 and then set off to return to us with a tent. They fell down so many crevasses they had to retreat as it was so dangerous. Ben told us about his journey back to base camp and what it was like meeting the other expedition on their way up.

It was then our turn. A strange thing had started to happen.

I found I could tell Ben everything. How close we had come to dying and how quietly scared we had all been, as it had felt like he had been there with us. But when it came to telling Lois, family or friends, I didn't think I could find the words to explain what happened. But an hour later I knew I would have to try.

Lois answered her phone in the gym.

'Ed, you're alive! We've been worried about you as we hadn't heard from you guys for so long.'

'Yeah, ummm, just about.'

'What do you mean "just about"?'

'Nothing, nothing. I'm all good. Everyone is fine. I've got to go. I love you and I'll give you a call when I get back to Kathmandu.'

That was all I could manage. I couldn't find the words to tell her in what would have to be a short conversation on the satellite phone. I decided to try again when we returned to Kathmandu the next day.

Even though we were all exhausted, there was also a feeling of elation. In the late afternoon, we crowded around Ben now we had more time to go into all the details, the endless crevasses, the snow conditions and how hard it all was. We didn't over-egg it, but he got the full version as we wanted him to realize how lucky he was not to have continued on with us. I didn't regret the experience of climbing further up Himlung, but it wasn't something I would want to necessarily repeat. There was much to learn from it and I could feel some of the changes were already beginning.

When the sun set, one of the porters put on music and there was a small party at base camp. We cracked open the bottle of rum I had brought with me and passed it around. In the starlight, we danced to Ben's favourite hip-hop songs and then switched to the Nepalis' much loved Bangalore tunes. The mishmash of cultures worked, as I always knew they had.

The following day, I woke from the best sleep I'd had in weeks. Being up high for so long, I had fully acclimatized to base camp's 4,900 metres and slept like a baby after fifty hours with pretty much no sleep. Around our last mountainside meal, we chatted with the Kenyan team who had tried to summit behind us. None of their six of climbers had managed to reach the top.

Soon, we were peering up at the sky, waiting for another helicopter to arrive. The one we had used the previous day had come with a hefty price tag of around £12,000, but our lives had depended on it and we were hopeful our insurance would cover it. The one we had scheduled today was booked months ago for a much more reasonable sum of $400 each. I had got the idea for a chopper exit back at Mera Peak three years before. When I had arrived back at base camp after that climb, I had looked on enviously as most of the people there were whisked away back to Kathmandu in helicopters. The last thing I wanted to do then was trek for five days when I was exhausted and scared of falling, but we hadn't arranged it in advance, so it wasn't an option. So when I researched the cost and realized you didn't have to be a millionaire, I secured places for the boys and Bigraj. It was a no-brainer to cut a week off our trip and ensure we all made it back safely and without any injuries.

We packed our kit up, our movements much slower than the last time we did it. We were all weak from the days without food or water; our faces chapped from sunburn and our limbs aching. We had decided to leave half our kit with the porters, who would take it back to Bigraj's office for him to store until I could return the following year.

Once finished, we went around to Kaji, Shyam, all the porters and guides, and thanked them for their help with our mission. Without them, there wouldn't have been an expedition, and we were grateful for their contribution. I knew I would be seeing them all again soon as I had decided to visit Nepal every year, whether with the beneficiaries of Millimetres 2 Mountains or on a solo adventure. While up in those snowy peaks, I realized I needed to prioritize what lit me up inside and I knew being in Nepal was part of that.

Again, we heard the chopper before we saw it. Within a few minutes, a larger helicopter with an enormous dragon emblazoned down the side set down in front of us. This time our pilot was Dutch, with a very dry sense of humour. Bigraj had already told us he owned a substantial commercial helicopter company in the Netherlands but still enjoyed coming out to do a season in Nepal for the scenery.

He sized us up before ushering us towards the back of the cab.

'I hope that is just insulation on you boys, because I've got my work cut out to get all five of you down the mountain. I might just have to take three of you down first.'

It was true that Arron and I were larger than your average mountaineer, but he managed to squeeze us in along with Bigraj, Ben and Beetle. Fortunately, he was a very experienced pilot and had already dropped some fuel at the region's capital to lighten his load. That was where we headed first.

Up we went, high above base camp, waving at everyone below until they were just specks. I then settled back for one of the best experiences of my life. We sped down the valley, tracing the river all the way, through large gullies with waterfalls on either side and feeling like kings of the world. All the beauty we had witnessed in the days of trekking was compressed and layered until I didn't think I could take much more.

After half an hour, we dropped down a massive canyon. I could understand why the pilot didn't want to carry unnecessary fuel on the way up. In less than half an hour, we had descended 1,800 vertical metres.

'Here's the capital of the region,' the pilot said, as we hovered over a village with no more than fifty houses. 'We just need to pick up some of the extra fuel and then we'll be off to Kathmandu. By the way, the Chief of Police has travelled in and was looking to speak with you.'

Oh. I couldn't imagine what we had done wrong.

'It will be because of the helicopter we took yesterday,' Bigraj explained.

As we landed, Bigraj told us that in recent years there had been issues with insurance fraud in Nepal. Some of the more dubious helicopter companies and guides had been in cahoots with each other. The guides would put their clients in unnecessary danger up in the mountains or pressurize the climbers to call helicopters when they weren't needed. Once the insurance was paid up, the guides would get a kickback from the helicopter company. It had become a multi-million-dollar scam and some of the largest insurers had threatened to pull out of Nepal if the government didn't act. A swift crackdown ensued and new directives were issued. I was shocked. I had always thought Nepal was such a safe and honest place. Everyone left their doors unlocked and nothing was ever pinched from your bag.

It would seem that in recent years, the lure of 'easy money' had dragged down a few in the largely reputable climbing community.

Once the helicopter landed, the pilot turned the engine off and I stepped out for the first time, not worrying about whether I would lose my head. A uniformed man was waiting for us. Despite his smiles, he quite obviously had 'police chief' stamped all over his demeanour.

He was very polite, friendly and full of Nepalese smiles, but we had clearly entered a mild interrogation scenario. All the helicopter requests were now monitored and checked out if they appeared dubious in any way. Because ours had dropped us at base camp and flown back to Kathmandu without any passengers, they wanted to check it was all 'above board'. Our pilot had wandered off to get his jerry cans of fuel and that left Bigraj, Arron and me to explain why we had needed the chopper the previous night. We told the police chief we were exhausted and delirious but not injured and that was why we needed the helicopter but not a hospital. It had been Arron who had first raised the possibility of a helicopter and he certainly wasn't in cahoots with one of the helicopter companies. The police chief gently probed our story and, eventually, we were allowed to go on our way.

A few hours later we were all outside The Mulberry Hotel. It felt like a lifetime ago that we had been there. I had forgotten what a busy city was like, with everyone intent on getting to wherever they needed to be without a spare second to soak up that very moment. We went straight to our bedrooms as each of us had only one thing on our minds: a hot rainforest shower.

I looked in the bathroom mirror as I waited for the water

to heat up, the first time I had seen myself in three weeks. My face was peeling off and I seemed to have aged five years, but I looked happy – my eyes were shining with life and adventure. It had all been worth it and I knew my skin would heal. The shower was calling to me, my first proper wash in weeks. I stood under the water for forty minutes, the dirt and grime circling the plughole until the water ran clean.

Sea bass. I wanted sea bass that evening if I could find it. Then, after dinner, I wanted to lie in a big, soft bed and sleep for twelve hours. I grinned to myself as I turned the shower off. At the very least, the mountains made you appreciate the small joys of life.

After the finest meal Thamel could offer, I spoke to Lois with the boys. None of us could find the words to explain more than the bare basics. I wasn't sure whether an ordeal so alien to everyday life would ever fully sink in. For the last couple of days, we had been on a massive high. We knew we had been through something special together and our bond was rock solid. Soon, we would have to go our separate ways and I knew returning to everyday life would be strange. I was already aware that the versions of the story I delivered would change depending on who I was talking to. My mum would get a heavily diluted version, implying we were fine the whole time and there was never anything to worry about. Lois would receive a version closer to the reality of the situation but with the riskier elements sanded away, while a few of my friends might get somewhere closer to the truth. But I knew I would find it difficult to fully talk about what really happened with anyone other than the people who were there. I decided that on the flight home, I would start to write about it. I had already kept journals for the first few weeks of the trip and needed to finish them.

After fourteen hours of much-needed sleep, I headed down to the hotel lobby to leave for the airport. I knew it wasn't enough to tackle the depths of my exhaustion, but I'd had the three things I craved the most: a shower, a decent meal and a good night's sleep. Life had simplified down to the necessities and that was just one of the changes I experienced during this next chance at life.

As always, Bigraj was there to greet us and accompany us to the airport. He was a little quiet on the journey and once we got to the airport, I pulled him aside to find out if anything was wrong. He had been away from his family for weeks and I wanted to check if all was well.

'Is everything okay, Bigraj?'

'Yes, yes, fine, thank you. Happy to have seen you and spent more time together.'

I didn't believe that everything was fine. I knew my friend pretty well and after a few more minutes of probing, he relented.

'I am sorry the trip was not a success,' he said quietly. 'I am sorry none of you summited.'

I grinned at him and grasped both of his shoulders.

'I know the tour operators in Nepal are fixated on summiting, but that is not what makes a successful trip, Bigraj.' He gave a small smile as I continued. 'How many times do I have to say it? It's about the journey, not the summit!'

He grinned back at me.

'And, my God, could we have asked any more of you? You got four pretty inexperienced climbers, two of whom have wonky legs, closer to the summit than the other two expedition teams. You put your life at risk for us twice. You saved our lives at least once. You saved Shyam's life too. And in the process, we had some of the most transformative weeks of our lives. If that doesn't equal success, I don't know what does!'

His grin finally reached his eyes.

'I'll be back next year,' I said. 'And we should start thinking about what we will climb together next.'

'Namaste, Ed,' Bigraj said.

He brought his hands to his forehead in the prayer sign and bowed his head.

'Namaste, Bigraj,' I said, mirroring his movements.

As we pushed our trolleys toward Departures, I turned to bring my hands up to my forehead in the prayer sign again. I knew I owed Bigraj my life and a plan was forming of how I could thank him.

CHAPTER 18

Two Years Later

'So, is everything set for the Scottish leg of the journey?' I asked Beetle.

He grinned into the camera. He was sitting in his parents' garden, enjoying the August evening sunshine.

'We're all set with a full itinerary. There will be salmon fishing and water skiing around a loch. You know, the more traditional Scottish pursuits.'

'Water skiing!' Ben exclaimed from his home in Norfolk. 'Really?'

'I thought it would be educational,' Beetle responded non-chalantly.

'Sounds good to me,' I said. 'Anything that is away from the norm.'

'Sorry, guys, I've got to go now. Wedding plans call,' said Arron. 'I'll see you tonight, Ed, for our pub dinner. And I'll see you two at the film premiere!'

'See you tonight, Arron.' I paused. 'Film premiere. It still sounds unreal. How did that happen?'

'Well, it was partly down to my epic footage,' Beetle said.

'And my stellar contribution,' Ben interjected.

'Don't forget Donkey Number 19. It gave it some heart,' Arron concluded.

I grinned at them. 'Yes, yes.'

They'd said it a hundred times, but it still made me smile.

'I'll see you all in two weeks at the *film premiere* in Edinburgh,' I said, about to sign off. 'Dress smart. No snowsuits. Arron, I'm talking to you. I know you've been waiting for a chance to jump back into that green number.'

I closed my laptop. Our regular catch-ups had started a few days after returning to the UK. We had quickly realized that not many people understood what we had been through and we could only really talk to each other about it. So, we decided to have a group video call.

On that first call, Beetle had proclaimed, 'Lads, I'm finding adjusting back to normal life far harder than climbing mountains. The only thing my mates want to talk about is cricket and I just want to talk about the meaning of life!'

We knew then that we had to make our calls a regular thing.

Two years had passed quickly and for a year, my friends had been contributing to a documentary, *The Mountain Within Me*, which traced the journey of my accident and recovery. It was partway through making the documentary that I climbed Himlung. Because of the events that had unfolded, the documentary makers asked to include some of it in the story and to use the footage Beetle took. So now Ben, Arron and Beetle had become part of the documentary, joining Lois, my family and friends in its making.

Our lives had moved on, but the bond the mountain had instilled in us had remained. Beetle's filmmaking career had skyrocketed and he had even begun leading his own adventure tours in Africa. Arron had taken his qigong work to new levels and more people, and I was set to attend his wedding in a couple of months. But it was Ben's journey that had been the most transformative.

If this had been a movie, Ben would have made it to the top of Himlung, perhaps with a flag in hand, proudly sinking it into the snow. A sign he had conquered his injuries and their outcome. But his story was more profound than that. Because sometimes our journey needs to be a realization that we *don't* need to do something to be happy within ourselves. We should be accepted just as we are and have nothing to prove to anyone. This is what Ben had done. He was a loving father and partner, with a second child on the way, and had set up a successful business. He could do that now because he was much more relaxed about life and what would happen next. He knew he was enough, was doing enough, and could allow life to unfold. Just like Arron described to us on the mountain, he had arrived at 'effortless action'.

As for me, one of my biggest learnings after my accident was the understanding that any plan you had could get torn up and thrown out of the window pretty quickly. I had been served that lesson on a golden plate with a sparkler on top when I was told I would probably never walk again. What Himlung had taught me was that I had started to stray away from my values and what lit me up inside and I needed to realign with that. For years, I had known there were two things I loved doing: working with the beneficiaries of my charity and climbing mountains. But neither of them paid a salary. In fact, they cost money. So, before climbing Himlung, I'd been sliding away from the things that brought me joy and towards doing the things that paid.

Once I returned from that expedition, I started turning down a lot of work, not because I didn't enjoy doing it, but because it wasn't entirely in line with what I knew I needed to focus on. The time away on Himlung to reassess and readdress had helped me realize I needed to put more of my energy into the charity and beneficiaries even though I didn't earn anything from it. The weird thing was that the more I learnt to say, 'Sorry, but I can't do that right now', the more paid work came in and I could pick what aligned more with my mission. The byproduct of not chasing money was that I made money. Once I took my attention away from driving relentlessly towards my goals and followed my gut and values instead, more doors opened. Life had a weird way of working out like that. Deep down, I had already known it. I just needed another hefty reminder to trust in it again. It may sound a little hippie, and perhaps it is, but it has served me well.

I stood up from my desk and stretched. I still used my old wheelchair as my desk chair – a reminder of what could have been. Coming from the kitchen were the sounds of Lois making sourdough so it could prove overnight and be ready to bake in the morning. Her love of creating the perfect loaf had continued through the past two years, much to my delight. I wandered through the cottage towards the kitchen to open a bottle of wine for us before we went out.

'So, I like a natural fermentation process,' Lois said from inside the kitchen. 'It takes a bit longer but I think the taste it produces is better.'

I paused outside the kitchen and smiled.

'And I am folding it gently enough?' came the other voice. 'I worry it is too hard.'

'No, no. You're doing a brilliant job.'

'Thank you, Lois.'

I stepped inside to join them. 'How are the two bakers doing?'

'Ed!' Bigraj said, his face lighting up. 'How are the boys?'

'They are all good. Pleased to see you earlier on the call.'

'Yes, I had to leave after a bit as Lois and I had got to a critical stage – the folding.'

'I have heard that it's the make-or-break stage of a loaf,' I said, with as much seriousness as I could muster. 'Ruin Lois' sourdough and you might as well book a flight home tomorrow.'

'It is a critical point,' he said, placing his hand in the bowl. 'See, you streeetch and fold. Streeetch and fold.'

'Very good!' Lois said, her eyes bright from finding a fellow enthusiast.

Bigraj had landed for his first trip abroad three days ago and he and Lois had fallen back into their familiar friendship. The biggest change was that we were now his 'guides', and it was our turn to show him our sights and ways of living. We had meticulously planned his trip so he could stay with various people around the country and explore all the UK had to offer. The previous year, I had taken a group, including a few of the beneficiaries of Millimetres 2 Mountains, to Nepal so they could experience trekking through the Manaslu region. There would be no more going up mountains with beneficiaries, but circling them was fully encouraged. Of course, Bigraj organized the whole tour with ease and a smile and consequently became friends with many of the people on it. When I had announced I had finally managed to arrange for him to come and stay with us, which was the idea I'd first had at the airport after Himlung, I was awash with offers to host him. Consequently, he was at the start of a Grand Tour fit for a Nepali Ambassador. He would soon be crisscrossing through the UK to stay at four locations in England and two in Scotland.

'By the way,' I said, as I headed over to the fridge to open a bottle of wine for us, 'Beetle has added salmon fishing and water skiing to the Scottish leg of the trip.'

'Water skiing!' Lois exclaimed.

'You sounded exactly like Ben,' I said as I handed her and Bigraj a glass of wine.

'You'll be staying with Beetle for three nights and then you'll both travel down to the film premiere in Edinburgh, where we'll all meet up.'

'And when is London?' Bigraj asked.

'That's next week, before Beetle,' I said from memory.

His itinerary was firmly implanted in my brain. Besides showing Bigraj a good time, the primary mission was not to lose him or send him off to the wrong city on the wrong day.

'Good. I look forward to seeing the cloud scratchers.'

I raised an eyebrow, unsure of his meaning.

'The umm . . . What is the word?' He thought for a moment. 'Skyscrapers! You call them skyscrapers. I call them cloud scratchers.'

I grinned. 'Fair enough. But don't get your hopes up. They're nowhere near as high as the natural "cloud scratchers" you have. In fact, you'll probably think of them as an average-sized hill. Wait until you experience the Underground though.'

When I started planning Bigraj's trip over a year ago, I knew there were two key things to it. First, Lois and I would pay for his flights and raise money for all his other expenses, as I knew he would never be able to spare the money for it. The second was I wanted him to have a trip of a lifetime. I was going large.

But as soon as he stepped off the airplane and Lois and I greeted him at the airport, I realized I had underestimated the impact of the simple cultural differences. After only a day, I realized how gloriously novel everything was to him, just as it was for me in Nepal.

He had taken to everything with gusto. The jetlag had barely touched him and he was up bright and early to explore with us every day. The first morning, we walked down a normal suburban pavement when I realized I was just talking to myself as Bigraj was no longer striding next to me. I turned around and he was ten metres behind, staring at the pavement. When I returned to get him, he told me the paving slabs had made him stop as he'd never seen anything as smooth and uniform. This continued over the days: the flatness of the roads, public libraries, ornate lampposts, the lack of dust, postboxes, fish and chips and our Aga all mesmerized him. They all drew him in as he appreciated their beauty or considered how they worked, why they were there or who they helped. It seemed that by stepping away from his norm, even if it was to walk down a street, he was on an adventure. It made me realize that adventure can come from whatever you like as long as you push yourself a bit further than the everyday. There doesn't have to be a high level of risk or any endangerment of life. It's just about stepping into the unknown for a while.

I left Lois and Bigraj to their baking and took my drink outside. Night was falling and we would soon take Bigraj out for a meal. We had found that he was a huge fan of gastro-pub cuisine, particularly the variety of meat on offer, and I was delighted to be his guide on that particular journey of exploration.

I settled down on my favourite bench that looked out across the fields and watched as the sun began to dip below the horizon. Soon, it would be dark and, as we lived in quite a remote part of the country, the stars would come out. Nothing even close to the delights I had stared up at in Nepal though.

I thought back to the night when I had seen the most brilliant display high above at 6,000 metres, the night when I didn't know whether it would be my last. Two years on, there were still no regrets.

If my first brush with death reframed my life and gave me perspective and purpose, my second brush with death made me realize how I had almost lost those gains. It also made me realize how much I didn't want to die. How much more there was for me to do with the charity. How much more *living* there was to do with Lois, my family and friends.

I had always raced through life with an element of risk by my side, right from when I was a boy diving too deep into the Egyptian sea, through to my chosen career in rugby. But brushing up against losing my life the second time made me realize I didn't want to put myself into positions where I might not survive. If Death had visited me during that long night on Himlung and asked me if I wanted to slip away with him, I would have politely, but very firmly, said no. If he had visited me in my hospital bed in intensive care, when I struggled alone at night to hold any hope of seeing my fingers or toes move again, I am not sure I would have been so firm in my refusal. I hadn't been able to picture the life I could build, but now I was living it.

In hindsight, some things could have been done differently on Himlung, but then again, there were always going to be hurdles. The situation on the mountain meant summiting was virtually impossible. We later found out there were seventeen attempts on Himlung that season with no successes. But even if I had known that in advance, I would have still gone. For me, the only purpose a summit now served was to motivate the journey, and what a journey we had been on. From the Battle of Besisahar to eating a snow leopard's leftovers, walking through deserted monasteries to meeting a monk, from rolling around laughing with Dil to spending a night under the stars above 6,000 metres, I was certain it would long remain one of the most incredible trips of my life and sharing it with my friends had made it all the more special.

The sun slipped below the horizon and I glanced back at the house, the light from the kitchen drawing my gaze. Through the window I could see Lois placing a bowl in the fridge, her task finally done. It would soon be time to go. I took another sip from my glass and leant back to enjoy the warmth of the night for a moment longer.

I was proud that I had turned around on Himlung when I had. I'd never had to consciously decide whether to stop trying to reach a goal when no one else was telling me to before. Over the years, I had always wondered whether I was strong enough to make the right decision, rather than stubborn enough to make the wrong one.

Our time on this planet is finite and how we choose to spend it is important. The night on the mountain was a necessary reminder of that. Turning around meant I got to celebrate not getting to the top for years to come. If I hadn't listened to the call to turn around and stepped away from the mountain's edge, that summit celebration would likely have been my last.

I now know my limits and what I am capable of and not many people can truly say that. Climbing Himlung was the hardest thing I have ever done – none of the other challenges I have set myself before or after have even come close. The level of output, exhaustion, effort and pain expanded my gauge. The barometer of what I can endure has had a few numbers added to its end and, consequently, what I can sustain for longer periods at lower altitudes has increased.

I'm often asked why I want to climb mountains. Why can't I resist their call? It is indeed a terrifyingly privileged experience that many might not understand. The answer is, I don't climb mountains to stand on top of them. It's for everything else they mean to me: the life-affirming experience, the challenge, isolation and realignment, being in nature, leaving my comfort zone and the relationships built and the bonds forged. But most of all, it is for the journey back to appreciating the present moment. Because if we are not present in our life, what is left?

Lois tapped at the window and I blinked open my eyes. The sun had set and it was time to return to the woman and the life that I loved.

ONE PLACE. MANY STORIES

Bold, innovative and
empowering publishing.

FOLLOW US ON:

@HQStories